Plant Based Diet

The ultimate plant-based diet meal plan with delicious vegan recipes for a healthy life | easy and ready-to-go meals, snacks and smoothies (vegan meal prep cookbook)

Table of Contents

Introduction

Congratulations on purchasing *Plant Based Diet: the ultimate plant-based diet meal plan with delicious vegan recipes for a healthy life – easy and ready-to-go meals, snacks and smoothies* and thank you!

The following chapters will cover everything you need to know about what it means to be vegan and how this lifestyle affects your health and well-being. The Alkaline Diet will be touched on also, as this is an important part of understanding how a vegan diet is so healthy. As you uncover the mechanics behind consuming whole, plant-based foods long term, the drive to incorporate this lifestyle into your diet will increase. So, to help you get started, this book details how to shop, what to look out for, the common pitfalls to avoid and tips and tricks to make transitioning into a vegan as easy as possible.

You will also find tons of vegan recipes that are sure to delight and satisfy. Everything from breakfast through to dessert and everything in between will be covered, including a variety of recipes that will meet you where you're at no matter your experience level. There are no-bake recipes with minimal ingredients and dishes to impress even the fussiest of dinner guests.

Within these pages, everything you need to know about becoming vegan will be delivered in an easy-to-digest manner, so you can move forward on your path to vibrant health, improved mood, better sleep, increased energy levels and longevity as quickly as possible.

If you finally want to learn a simple way to reclaim the optimal health you deserve, don't forget to buy the most famous Daisy Evans book:

ALKALINE DIET: body balance and metabolism reset for an incredible healthy living (increase energy and reverse disease with delicious recipes, smoothies and herbal medicine secrets for beginners)

Chapter 1: Veganism. What is it and how can it improve my life?

What does vegan mean? Put very simply, it is a diet that contains no animal products, meaning nothing that comes from an animal in any way ends up on a vegan's plate. This includes meat, milk, cheese, eggs, and honey. If an animal had anything to do with making the food item, it is not included in this diet.

Reasons to go Vegan

There are different sub-categories of vegans and different reasons that the millions of vegans today have chosen this lifestyle. Every person's choices and reasons are individual to them, as yours will be to you, but here are some of the most common reasons to give up animal products in your diet.

- **Dietary Vegan**: This person has chosen to give up all animal products from their diet primarily for the health and well-being of their body. In today's culture, the average person consumes far more animal products than were ever intended for the body to be able to process. This high percentage of meat, eggs, and dairy becomes a burden on the body to break down, and this results in weight-gain, liver congestion, systemic inflammation, cardiovascular disease, metabolic disease, digestive issues, gallbladder disease, skin issues, lethargy, sleep issues, and general malaise. Dairy and eggs are two of the most common dietary allergens that people suffer from today and are the cause of a lot of digestive disturbances and on-going health issues that affect the population. These allergens can go undiagnosed for years, causing many of the above issues.

Upon researching these issues, this person decides to remove all animal products from their diet in hopes of improving their health, managing a disease, avoiding allergic reactions or discomfort, or increasing their longevity. For the purposes of this book, this is the type of vegan that we will be focusing on and the health issues mentioned above will be explored further throughout the following pages.

- **Ethical Vegan**: This person has chosen to abstain from all animal products due to opposing the exploitation of animals. Unfortunately, the animals that provide the products that line our supermarket shelves are not given the choice to do so. Due to the enormous amount of such products demanded by society, the treatment of these animals suffers in the supply-and-demand chain of events to get the meat, eggs, and dairy to the billions of supermarkets and restaurants around the world. 'Humane' slaughtering methods of animals are impossible to monitor and sustain in an industry as immense as the meat and dairy sector and so inevitable short cuts are made that mean an often torturous, traumatizing and horrific end to these animal's lives.

The vast majority of these animals suffer from the moment they are born until they are slaughtered for their meat. This is a very basic overview of the standards within the meat and dairy industry, but much, much more information is available for those who want to learn more. Once uncovering these truths, an ethical vegan removes all animal products from their diet and their wardrobe in an effort to boycott the meat and dairy industry and remove themselves from this cruel chain of supply and demand.

- **Environmental Vegan**: This person avoids all animal products due to the impact that industrial animal farming has on the environment. This industry is extremely damaging to the environment and is 100% unsustainable. It impacts the Earth by way of:
    o soil acidification

- water wastage
- deforestation
- eutrophication
- greenhouse gas emissions

The sheer number of animals needed to supply this industry with products means that 30% of the world's ice-free surface is used to contain and support them (70% of all agricultural land), while 45% of croplands go to the feeding of these animals. This causes deforestation issues and impacts habitat for wild animals and the balance of the eco-system.

Raising, cleaning after, feeding and slaughtering animals uses an astronomical amount of water resulting in nearly 2.5 thousand gallons of water being used to produce 1 single pound of meat. The run-off water from these facilities then pollutes the surrounding land and areas which affects nutrients in the soil and kills aquatic life in nearby ponds and lakes. Also, the excessive amounts of hormones used to speed the growth, milk and egg production of these animals end up in their fecal matter, which also pollute the ground and local water sources, negatively affecting animal and human life that come into contact with it.

Industrial animal farming is responsible for nearly 20% of the world's greenhouse gas emissions, including nitrous oxide, carbon dioxide, and methane. This is more than every single transport system in the world combined. Per person, a meat-eater contributes seven times as much greenhouse gas emissions than a vegan from the food they purchase.

The meat and dairy industry cause more damage to the Earth than any other industry. People that are conscious of this, forgo all animal products from their lifestyle in an effort to off-set these statistics. One person replacing one meat-based meal per day with a vegan meal for just one week would have the same impact on the environment as not driving their car for five full weeks.

What am I giving up?

When you go vegan, you're giving up all meat, dairy, and eggs. At first, this can seem very daunting, but so long as you find similar replacements, the transition is not as difficult as it seems. There are many vegan product replacements you can use, but some of these can be almost as unhealthy as the products you are trying to replace. Vegan cheeses and meats vary in both quality and nutrient value, so finding the products that work the best for you is important. But, as you progress through this book, you will learn about the many wholefoods, home-made options there are for your meat, cheese and dairy intake which will not only remove the toxins you are eating but replace them with health-promoting ingredients.

For example, replacing the meat, cheese, and mayo you would use to make a cheeseburger with a cheap store-bought veggie burger patty, vegan cheese slices, and vegan mayonnaise, would remove the cholesterol, majority of saturated fat and increase the fiber content slightly, but it wouldn't boost the health factor exponentially. But learning how to make a bean patty, vegan cheese sauce and home-made vegan mayo would boost the nutrient content and decrease the toxic load from the original cheeseburger by a long shot.

It is relatively easy to be a junk-food vegan as the amounts of vegan brands and products out there are many and varied. Learning how to transition into a vegan lifestyle with the emphasis being on improving your health and well-being is a slightly different path to take, but one that will see you reach a better version of you much quicker.

The history of how our diets got to be so animal-based
Originally, meat and animal products of butter, cheese, milk, and eggs, were very health-promoting to civilizations that worked very hard and struggled to flourish. Humans spent a lot of time and energy hunting and gathering food, and with all this energy expenditure, meat and dairy held the most benefits to replace what was lost in their exerted lifestyle. But the quantity of the animal products that were eaten was far different than today. One animal

would feed many, many people and a single meal would contain a very small portion of meat to the larger portions of grains and vegetables. The animal's bones and organs would flavor large stews of plant-based ingredients so that every last piece of the animal would go to feeding the people.

As humanity progressed and the industrial revolution made things easier and faster to obtain, both the quality and quantity of these animal products suffered. The animals were free-roaming and wild with natural instincts and behaviors providing them with the knowledge of what to eat for their own health and wellbeing. Their daily grazing habits kept them fit and lean, but the industrial revolution saw an end to this with animals being kept in cages and fed a diet similar to the one that is causing so many complications amongst humans. A diet high in processed carbohydrates and corn, growth hormones and medications, being over-fed to have them produce as much extra meat as possible in the shortest amount of time, and not being allowed to burn the weight off with exercise. These animals are not in great health when they are slaughtered, in fact, they are suffering from the same metabolic syndrome that their meat is causing humans to suffer from. Coupled with the heavy toxic load they carry from this lifestyle, those who eat this animal's meat are not only consuming something far different to what our ancestors hunted, but they are also consuming far too much of it. Eggs, pork, butter and processed wheat for breakfast, followed by a chicken, bacon and mayo sandwich for lunch and then a red meat roast for dinner smothered in gravy with a side of cream and butter laden potatoes. Our ancestors would have balked at the gross over-indulgence we consider normal today. Our digestive systems were never meant to cope with so many different animals cooked with so much fat and dairy in one day. No wonder there are so many health complications today!

But we've always eaten meat, it's natural and good for us!
The human body developed to be an omnivore, meaning that it is able to process a wide variety of both plant and animal-based foods. This mechanism is purely for survival as we are unable to consume foods in the same way that true carnivores do. Our teeth are not sharp enough to pierce the hide of a cow and our digestive tract and immune system are not as strong as true carnivores. We are able to digest and break-down cooked meat with relative ease, but our immune system and stomach acids are not equipped to deal with the bacteria and pathogens found in a wild raw meat

environment on a long-term basis. Also, in order to extract as many nutrients as possible from our food, our intestines are made with millions of little folds that increase the surface area of the intestines as the food passes through it. Carnivore animals do not have these folds, their intestines are smooth so that the high amounts of meat and organs they consume slide through easily without getting stuck. A human eating a high-meat diet does not have this luxury however, and meat, fat and grease get caught in these folds, impacting the intestines and colon which decreases their ability to absorb essential nutrients and puts their internal health at risk as this food is not excreted by the body and instead begins to rot internally.

We also developed our molars to help us grind down our highly fibrous vegetables and beans, and our digestive bacteria which are highly essential to our health, are fed by these very fibrous foods. This shows that we are primarily developed to be herbivores but are also able to digest small quantities of meat.

What are the health implications of eating meat and dairy?

Diets high in meat and animal products have been proven to put a huge strain on our system like the heavy amounts of cholesterol, fat and another being's toxic load become too hard for our stomach to break down and our liver to process in a timely manner. Decreased amounts of fiber mean that our microbiota suffers, and bad bacteria begins to flourish within. Decreased amounts of fresh fruits and vegetables mean that our nutritional profile diminishes, and the functioning of our nervous system becomes less equipped to enable communication between our organs, brain, and muscles. It is not only the meat that we eat however, but it is also all the other food that goes with it. Our meat today is cooked with an excess of salt and saturated fats to make it as tasty as possible and it is served with processed foods as the sides, dressings, and accompaniments. Heavy mayo, creamy sauces, deep-fried appetizers, sugary and processed bread alongside big glasses of pop leave our bodies heaving with toxins and overwhelmed with the sheer enormity of processed junk.

Gone are the days of eating a whole-foods diet that was gathered fresh that morning from the land. Gone are the days of having sensibly portioned meals that don't leave us feeling so full that we can barely move. Our bodies are suffering, our medical systems are overwhelmed with diseased patients, people are dying from obesity and cardiovascular-related issues.

And the reasons are simple: the more of this unnatural diet we consume and sedentary lifestyle we live, the less chance we have to thrive as once intended. It is affecting us in the following ways:

- o **Fiber content** – we are not getting enough soluble and insoluble fiber from a diet high in meat and processed sugars. Our healthy microbiota is being killed off by bacteria that are making us sick.

- **Glycemic load** – our pancreas is overwhelmed with the lack of slow-burning, whole-foods and complex carbohydrates. When the pancreas suffers, diabetes sets in, and we become insulin-dependent to cope with the digestion of our food.

- **Poor macronutrient composition** – our balance of complex carbohydrates, clean protein, and healthy fats is twisted into a diet high in saturated fats, excess toxic meats, and processed carbohydrates. There is nothing of health for the body to hold onto, so it becomes overwhelmed with an excess of disease-inducing foods that it is unable to process and instead is forced to store as fat to keep it out of the system.

- **Low micronutrient density** – a diet low in fruits, vegetables, nuts, seeds, and legumes means our bodies are not getting what they need in the form of vitamins, minerals, and phytochemicals. Its store of these essential vitamins and minerals begin to dwindle, our organs and body systems are unable to function at an optimal level and our bodies become further ill-equipped to cope with the processed diet we are still piling into our digestive system.

- **Poor fatty acid composition** – Our fat cells are designed to store fat away from our internal organs to use when we come into periods where there is a lack of food. The types of fats we consume will determine whether the fat we carry in storage is 'good fat' or 'bad fat'. Good fats are things like omega 3 and 6 which are called essential fatty acids, meaning they are essential to the body for good health. Monounsaturated fats are also a good source of fat, defined by the way the body is able to break them down and use them, and we find these fats in things like avocado, nuts, and coconuts. Bad fats are trans fats which are found in animal products, processed foods, margarine, processed oils, deep-fried foods, and most pre-packaged meals. Trans fats are toxic and disease-inducing and act like a poison in our system. Saturated fats aren't always bad when in their whole and natural forms and are okay to be consumed in small amounts. In short, good fats are disease preventing and bad fats are disease inducing.

- **Sodium-Potassium ratio** – Potassium is naturally found in plants and sodium is naturally found in animals. Potassium is essential to the body because it is involved in fluid balance at a cellular

16

level and supports healthy blood pressure. Sodium is important because it is involved in fluid balance at an extracellular level and it also plays a role in nutrient absorption and nerve and muscle communication. These micronutrients work closely within the body, and when they are out of balance, catastrophic things begin to happen with an increased risk of kidney disease, stroke, heart failure, some cancers, and high blood pressure. It is essential that the balance of potassium and sodium is maintained, and we do this by decreasing the amount of sodium-rich foods like meat, processed foods, and packaged meals and increase the amount of potassium-rich foods like fresh fruits, vegetables, and grains.

- o **Acid-base balance** – This will be explained further in the following chapter, but essentially this is the alkaline/acid pH balance in the body and how it impacts our health and our ability to function at an optimal level. Highly acidic foods are meats, dairy, and processed foods and sugars. Highly alkaline foods are vegetables and fruits and 'clean' proteins.

Cholesterol

Cholesterol is only found in animals and humans. Plants do not produce cholesterol. If you are concerned about high cholesterol or have a family history of high cholesterol, the best thing you can do for your health is to go vegan.

Cholesterol is essential to the human body for the creation of cell membranes and bile acids. It plays a crucial role in hormone production and fat-soluble vitamins like A, D, E and K. These vitamins are stored in the body and they wouldn't be able to do so without cholesterol. The human body makes enough of its own cholesterol to perform these vital roles and cholesterol is not a bad thing! It only becomes bad when we consume too much of another animal. Our bodies are unable to deal with this excess of product and it begins to build up in our arteries and blood vessels, which is a major contributing factor to heart disease and stroke.

Removing cholesterol from your diet will give your body a chance to regain its cholesterol balance, and eating high fiber and antioxidant-rich foods will help your body clear out the excess cholesterol that's stuck.

What about protein?

This is the number one argument you will hear in the transition to becoming vegan. The protein that everyone is so worried about is meat, as there is a gross misconception that this is the only source of protein, but this is incredibly false.

A protein is made up of twenty amino acids, nine of which are considered essential because we are unable to produce them ourselves in our bodies. This means we have to get them from outside sources. There are many ways to get these essential amino acids, and they are broken up into two protein groups:

- **Complete proteins** – put simply, these are proteins that contain all of the essential amino acids that make up a whole protein. These complete proteins are found almost entirely in animals and animal products.

- **Incomplete proteins** – these are plant proteins that are made up of some of the essential amino acids, but not all. Plant proteins are classified as incomplete proteins because you have to marry them together for them to become 'complete' but doing so is easy and delicious.

So why not just eat complete meat proteins then? Because while your body is working to pull out the complete proteins from the meat in your digestive tract, it is also working overtime to process all the cholesterol, fat and toxins that are also in the meat. Most plant proteins may have to be combined to become whole, but in breaking down these whole fruits, vegetables, and legumes, your body is also gaining a host of other nutrient-rich products such as fiber, vitamins, minerals, and phytochemicals.

Now, there are some amazing complete plant foods that are considered exceptional in their protein content. These are as follows:

- Quinoa
- Organic soy or tempeh
- Hemp hearts
- Chia seeds
- Spirulina
- Buckwheat

To help make incomplete plant proteins simple, here is a small chart to go by showing the main three amino acids that plant proteins need to be married with.

Plant Protein	Missing Amino Acid	Found in
Nuts and seeds	Lysine	Beans and legumes
Beans and legumes	Methionine	Whole grains Seeds and nuts Corn and rice
Rice and grains	Lysine	Beans and legumes
Corn	Lysine Tryptophan	Beans and legumes

So, by following the guide above, it's pretty easy to see what you have to do to get a complete protein in your meal. Beans and legumes should always be eaten with nuts or seeds, rice or corn, or any kind of whole grain. Nuts and seeds (to become a complete protein) should be eaten with a bean or legume, and so on. Some good examples are as follows:

- **Complete protein plant meals:**
  - Beans and rice – Salad greens with chickpea and black bean mixture, red onion, diced tomato, avocado, wild rice, peas, and an Italian vinaigrette
  - Quinoa salad – quinoa with diced salad veg, avocado, sunflower seeds, and a tahini lemon dressing
  - Pumpkin seed butter – pumpkin seed butter drizzled on a whole wheat cracker with a sprinkle of salt.
  - Hummus with whole grain crackers and vegetables – chickpea hummus, a sprinkling of sesame seeds and served with baby carrots, celery sticks and whole grain crackers to dip
  - Rice noodles with black beans and peanut satay – noodle stir-fry with a peanut satay sauce, black beans, snow peas, grated carrot, fresh ginger, and sesame seeds
  - Lentil soup with barley – vegetable broth with red lentils, barley, vegetables, spices, and fresh herbs.
  - Peanut butter on whole wheat bread – doesn't get any better than a PB and J.

o Tofu stir-fry – your favorite Asian vegetables, a beautiful teriyaki sauce, some sesame seeds, tofu, and mung bean sprouts

So, put simply, how can going vegan improve my health? When you decide to give up animal products you are saying goodbye to a host of health issues that come along with this lifestyle, including:

- Heart disease
- Stroke
- Atherosclerosis
- Diabetes
- Metabolic syndrome
- Gout
- High cholesterol
- Hypertension
- Colon cancer
- Gallbladder disease
- Liver congestion
- Obesity

And that is just to name a few. Today's meat is not what it should be and consuming these products means welcoming all the disease that the animal had before being slaughtered as well as the potential disease that your own body is unable to avoid.

Eating vegan means eating clean, whole foods that come from the ground where the soil provides rich minerals that you wouldn't be able to get any other way. Phytochemicals that plants make to protect themselves against danger will also help your own body fight off diseases including cancer, heart disease, and metabolic syndrome. Phytochemicals are plant medicine and eating whole plants is your best way to consume this powerful disease prevention before you ever get to a diseased state. Plants are exceptionally high in fiber that feed the good bacteria in our bodies who in turn keep the bad bacteria at bay. Bad bacteria prevent our bodies from breaking down and absorbing nutrients, feeding off our food for themselves. They also produce off-gases and waste as they feed, essentially poisoning our bodies from the inside.

All the vitamins and minerals you could ever hope to get come from plants, fruits, and vegetables. Plants do not contain trans fats, they only contain good fats. Eating vegan reduces your risk of cancer and protects against chronic disease. Bone, heart and cognitive health are supported and maintained with a vegan lifestyle.

Chapter 2: The Alkaline Diet: Why it is Important for Optimal Health

The Alkaline Diet is based on the theory that every food we eat, once digested, leaves ash similar to that of a fire behind that our body has to deal with. Food falls into two categories of alkaline inducing foods and acid-inducing foods. Our body is too alkaline or acidic one way or the other is potentially life-threatening, so the main hypothesis of this diet is that by decreasing the foods that cause acidity in the body and increasing the alkaline-inducing foods instead, our bodies will find a balance and rediscover true health and vitality.

Alkaline foods: These are fruits, vegetables, legumes, nuts, and seeds.

Acid foods: These are meat, meat products, processed sugars, bread, baked goods, alcohol.

The misconception about this diet is that these foods are able to change the pH of the blood, but this is near impossible. The body keeps a very, very tight hold over the pH of the blood, as it shifting by a few decimal points can mean the difference between life and death. The pH that is actually affected is the pH of the body, in the interstitial space and in the fluids.

As discussed previously, the food we eat today is far different than the food of our ancestors. The industrial revolution and factory farming have affected the mineral content of our soils and the highly processed diet we consume is lacking in whole foods and has excessive levels of sodium and trans fats. The diet of today is considerably low in potassium, yet high in sodium, proteins, processed grains, and refined sugars. All of these acid-forming foods leave the body in a situation where it has to buffer the damage that acidity causes. These issues start with generalized inflammation as the body is alerted to the increased acidic load.

The kidneys are primarily responsible for maintaining the electrolyte levels of our fluids, where they are used to buffer acidity and inflammation in the body. The main electrolytes that are used to keep the body in a state of pH balance are calcium, sodium, magnesium, and potassium. They all work in a give and take scenario. The best mineral to combat acidity is calcium, and as the calcium of the blood is also tightly regulated by the body, the kidneys then signal for calcium to be taken from the bones to buffer the acidity and escort it from the body via urine.

Now here is where the real evidence of the Alkaline Diet comes into effect. Researchers found that when someone eats a diet high in acid-forming foods, they are able to measure the acidity by way of the output of minerals in the urine. They found when someone switched to an alkaline diet, the urine becomes neutral, meaning there are no mineral imbalances occurring in the body.

Along with this urine evidence, the instance of other health issues was documented. Those who consumed a high acid diet had higher instances of osteoporosis due to the calcium being leeched from their bones.

People also suffered from hypertension due to the excess sodium in their blood in conjunction with atherosclerosis from high cholesterol levels. When blood pressure is raised, the sheer force of the blood puts a lot of pressure on the blood vessels. Eventual damage happens on the inside of the vessels that the cholesterol in the blood begins to stick to. More and more cholesterol cling onto this damaged part as the blood flows through until you eventually have plaque formations that begin to occlude the blood vessel. This is the progression of atherosclerosis from a diet high in sodium and cholesterol.

This same research found that acidic diets coincided with elevated levels of chronic pain and inflammation. This mainly affected people by way of joint pain, headaches, back pain, muscle cramps, and extreme menstrual pain. A higher risk of cancer and heart disease was also noted due to the fact that acidity in the body compromises mineral and vitamin absorption which leaves the body defenseless against outside pathogens. In this case, there is an accumulation of toxins that become a burden on the body and the immune system is weakened, leaving cancer to grow without being targeted on time and letting heart disease manifest without any antioxidant support. People in this category also suffered from obesity and obesity-related illnesses.

When people switched to an alkaline diet however, they had none of the above symptoms. Their urine was neutral, and their bone and muscle health improved. High blood pressure was lowered due to the consumption of more potassium and no sodium. Cholesterol levels went down due to no more cholesterol in the diet. Chronic pain was reported as either significantly decreased or gone altogether. Vitamin and mineral levels returned to very healthy levels and their risk of cardiovascular disease decreased.

The Alkaline Diet is still being researched for more concrete ways of testing the theory. But the evidence speaks for itself with the number of success stories from people who have turned their lives and health journeys around after trying it. Of course, eating more whole plant foods will have a positive impact on the body, but the specifics of this diet are very interesting and make a lot of sense. The mechanics behind eating a diet high in processed foods and meats and the related health issues are laid out clearly with this diet. Understanding how metabolic acidosis impacts our ability to thrive is another step in the direction of going vegan for better health and wellbeing.

If you want to deepen this topic, please refer to the book ***ALKALINE DIET: body balance and metabolism reset for an incredible healthy living (increase energy and reverse disease with delicious recipes, smoothies and herbal medicine secrets for beginners)***
-available only on Amazon-

You will learn the scientific approach to understand pH and its effects on your physical and mental health, the foods that silently influence your wellbeing and how to reset your metabolism to experiment new levels of energy, with immediate effect.

Chapter 3: Understanding Plant Micronutrients

Plants are rich in micronutrients that come from the soil they grow in, the basics of life they need to grow, the phytochemicals they use to protect themselves, attract insects and adapt to the changes around them. As plants are unable to move as animals do, they have a uniquely full tool chest of macro and micro-nutrients that enable them to adapt to the changing environment around them. These micronutrients are just as valuable to humans as they are to the plants but in different ways.

Below is a breakdown of the basic micronutrients found in fruits, vegetables, nuts, seeds, and legumes.

Vitamins

Vibrant vegetables and fruits are a dense source of vitamins that are essential to overall health and wellness.

- Vitamin A: Also known as beta-carotene is a carotenoid found in yellow, orange and dark green fruits and veg, most notably carrots, spinach, and broccoli. It protects against infections and is essential for eye and skin health.
- Vitamin Bs: This group of vitamins is responsible for maintaining the nervous system and cognitive function, DNA and blood cell production.
    - 1 is responsible for nervous system health and aids in the breakdown and absorption of food. Found in peas, whole grains, and most fruits and vegetables.
    - 2 is responsible for energy production and healthy skin and eyes and found in asparagus, spinach, and broccoli.
    - 3 is great for healthy skin and energy production and is found in peanuts, avocados, peas, and mushrooms.
    - 6 is also essential for energy production and is found in chickpeas, potatoes, banana, squash, and nuts.
    - 9 is also known as folate and is essential for fetal development and growth and healthy cell division. It is found in legumes, asparagus, spinach, arugula, kale, and beets.
    - 12 is predominantly sourced from animal products but you can find it in some organic soy products but most notably nutritional yeast.

- Vitamin C: An essential vitamin important for cell growth and energy production as well as tissue repair and wound healing. It is one of the most powerful antioxidants and is found in strawberries, spinach, Brussel sprouts, sweet potatoes, and tomatoes.
- Vitamin E: A powerful antioxidant that protects the body from free radical damage including premature aging. It's of great support to the immune system, protecting it against external pathogens. It is found in sunflower seeds, almonds, hazelnuts, spinach, and broccoli.
- Vitamin K: This vitamin plays a major role in the clotting cascade and also in bone health. It is found in all green leafy veg as well as cruciferous veg and green tea.

Minerals

- **Macro-minerals:** we need these in large quantities from our diet.
    - Calcium: This essential mineral plays roles in bone, heart, muscle and nerve health. Foods high in calcium are spinach, collard greens, seeds, almonds, soybeans, and butter beans.
    - Chloride: This mineral plays a part in body fluid balance including digestive juices. It is found in sea salt, tomatoes, lettuce, celery, and rye bread.

- o Magnesium: This mineral regulates blood sugar and assists in energy production. It also helps your muscles, kidneys, bones and heart function effectively. It is found in spinach, quinoa, dark chocolate, almonds, avocado, and black beans.
- o Phosphorous: This mineral is found in bones and works with calcium in maintaining healthy mineral balance within the body. It is found in pumpkin, sunflower seeds, lentils, chickpeas, oatmeal, and quinoa.
- o Sodium: The current population gets excess sodium from all pre-packaged foods and restaurant meals, so there is no need to go looking for extra sodium in the diet.
- o Potassium: This mineral is essential in blood pressure balance, muscle health, and nerve function. It is found in avocado, bananas, apricots, grapefruit, potatoes, mushrooms, cucumbers and zucchini.

- **Trace Minerals:** We just need tiny amounts of these from our foods.
  - o Copper: Essential in the formation of red blood cells and iron absorption. It is found in whole grains, beans, potatoes, cocoa, black pepper, and dark leafy greens.

- Cobalt: This trace mineral works closely with B12 in the formation of hemoglobin. It is found in nuts, broccoli, oats, and spinach.
- Manganese: Plays many roles in enzyme activity and cellular level antioxidants. It is found in pineapple, peanuts, brown rice, spinach, sweet potato, pecans, and green tea.
- Iodine: Essential for thyroid function, you can find it in seaweed, lima beans, and prunes.
- Iron: Used to make hemoglobin and as a carrier for essential nutrients in the blood. In plant form, it is found in cashews, spinach, whole grains, tofu, potatoes, and lentils.
- Selenium: A trace mineral essential in the role of reproduction, DNA production, and antioxidant function. It is found in brazil nuts, lentils, cashew nuts, and potatoes.
- Zinc: As your body doesn't store zinc, it needs to be consumed daily because it plays important roles in nutrient metabolism, immune system maintenance, and enzyme function. It is found in legumes, nuts, seeds, potatoes, kale and green beans.

Colors

The colors in fruits and vegetables point to what kinds of nutrients they contain.

- White foods: Contain sulfur and can have anti-cancer properties. Found in cauliflower, garlic, leeks, and onions.
- Green foods: Contain lutein and vitamin K. Found in dark leafy greens, broccoli, avocado.
- Purple foods: Contain anthocyanins, which are powerful antioxidants. Found in blueberries, eggplant, red cabbage, and blackberries.
- Red foods: Contain lycopene and has therapeutic properties for the heart. Found in strawberries, watermelon, tomatoes, and red bell peppers.

Chapter 4: Vegan Super Foods

To be clear, most superfoods are already vegan, but there are some that are particularly high in nutrient content. The following are the top vegan superfoods available today. These should be incorporated into your diet every chance you get. The following are twelve of the best superfoods that you will find at your local grocery store.

1. **Dark Leafy Greens**

Kale, swiss chard, spinach, and collard greens are all classed as dark leafy greens and these superfoods should be incorporated into your daily meal plan. Not only are they a great digestive aid due to their high fiber content, but they're also dense sources of vitamins C and K, zinc, calcium, magnesium, iron and folate. They have a high antioxidant profile that assists the body in removing harmful free radicals which in turn reduces the risk of cancer, heart disease, and stroke.

2. **Berries**

Natures little antioxidants are also the most delicious and delicate fruits we know. Berries host an array of benefits to the body and each one has its own special powers:

- o Strawberries contain more vitamin C than oranges! They are antioxidant rich and provide us with fiber, potassium, anthocyanins, and folate. Strawberries reduce the risk of cancer, are supportive in the control of diabetes, and are great anti-inflammatories.
- o Blueberries are one of the most antioxidant-rich foods out there. They contain manganese and vitamins C and K, are supportive of cognitive function and mental health.
- o Raspberries are rich in vitamin C, selenium and phosphorus. Research shows they are beneficial in controlling blood sugar in diabetics. They are a great source of quercetin that is known to slow the onset and growth of cancer cells.
- o Blackberries are incredibly high in antioxidants and fiber and are loaded with phytochemicals that fight cancer. They are also packed with vitamin C and K.

3. Nuts and Seeds

Nuts and seeds are a vegan's best friend when it comes to texture, variety, healthy fats, and proteins. They are incredibly nutrient dense and contain excellent levels of fats, protein, complex carbs, fiber. They are loaded with vitamins and minerals that are easily absorbed and fun to eat, while at the same time helping to protect our bodies against disease. Every nut and seed have their own special traits:

- o Pine nuts have an excess amount of manganese.
- o Brazil nuts are the leading source of selenium
- o Pistachios are well known for their lutein content that supports eye health
- o Almonds and sunflower seeds are great sources of vitamin E.
- o Cashews have more iron than any other food in this category.
- o Pumpkin seeds are one of the best possible sources of zinc.

4. Olive Oil

A staple of the Mediterranean diet for a reason, this oil is rich in antioxidants and monounsaturated fats that support cardiovascular health, prevent strokes and feed your hair and skin like nothing else. Despite being fat, it actually supports healthy weight maintenance.

5. **Mushrooms**

The best vegan meat source there is but they're low in calories while being high in protein and fiber. They're a great source of B vitamins, vitamin D, potassium and selenium. They are high in antioxidants, support healthy gut bacteria and are beneficial in weight loss.

6. **Seaweed**

Used in medicine for centuries, seaweed has antiviral properties and has recently tested positively in killing certain cancer cells. Seaweed benefits cholesterol levels and is rich in antioxidants that are proven to lower the instance of heart disease. Seaweed is incredibly rich in vitamin A, C, D, E and K, and also B vitamins. It's brimming with iron and iodine which is essential for thyroid function, as well as having decent amounts of calcium, copper, potassium, and magnesium.

7. **Garlic**

Garlic is a powerful medicinal ally to have on hand. It is rich in vitamins B6 and C, but most importantly, it boosts immune function, lowers blood pressure, improves cholesterol levels and supports cardiovascular health. Fresh garlic is brimming with antioxidants that have a potent effect on overall health.

8. **Avocado**

Avocado is a great source of MUFAs (Mono-Unsaturated Fatty Acids) which is a huge factor in cardiovascular function. They support vitamin and mineral absorption, healthy skin, hair, and eyes, improved digestive function and also contains twenty vitamins and minerals. Avocados provide anti-inflammatory activity and are loaded with soluble fiber.

9. Turmeric

Highly anti-inflammatory and has potent anti-cancer properties. It has been shown to provide pain relief in arthritic conditions and supports liver health due to its high antioxidant levels. Turmeric can be hard to absorb however so taking it with black pepper improves its absorptivity.

10. Chia Seeds

These tiny seeds are packed full of omega 3 fatty acids, in fact, they are one of the best vegan sources out there. They are also antioxidant rich and packed with protein, calcium, iron and soluble fiber. Due to this, they are recommended to reduce the occurrence of cardiovascular disease, diabetes, and obesity. They are healing to the digestive tract, contribute to feelings of fullness so support weight loss, they can help lower cholesterol and best of all, when mixed with water, they make a great egg substitute.

11. Legumes

A study was conducted that investigated what the longest living people and cultures in the world had in common. The only dietary thing they shared was that legumes were a huge part of their diet, in fact, the longest living people in the world at these every day. Legumes are rich in protein, fiber, and complex carbohydrates but also contain potassium, magnesium, folate, iron, B vitamins, zinc, copper, manganese, and phosphorus. These little guys are highly nutritious and loaded with soluble fiber that benefits colon health, feed healthy bacteria and reduce the risk of colon cancer.

12. **Spirulina**

Spirulina is a blue-green alga that is brimming with vitamins, minerals, and antioxidants. Algae is the greens of the sea and pack the same benefits as vegetables of the land in terms of being nutrient dense, but something about growing under the sea makes them like the Superman of vegetables. They are a great supplemental form of protein but also contain potassium, magnesium, calcium, iron, phosphorous, vitamins A and C. They benefit the cardiovascular system by lowering the risk of cholesterol and high blood pressure. They also play a role in mental health by supporting serotonin production while working simultaneously to help eliminate heavy metals and toxins from the body.

Chapter 5: Let's Go Shopping

Now that we have a good understanding of the nutritional value of plant-based foods, let us go to the supermarket to stock the cupboards, fridge, and freezer with everything we need to get this new lifestyle started.

Every supermarket is laid out in a similar way, so this list will be designed to make it as easy as possible for you to get what you need and navigate the layout with ease. There will always be a fresh produce section which usually is the first area you come across but is sometimes the last. It is always to one side of the supermarket. The dairy fridges are usually close by to the produce, along with the vegetarian fridges. The health foods aisle will be adjacent to the produce section along with the bulk bins.

The middle aisles of the supermarket are always reserved for convenience and junk foods, cereals, and packet meals. The personal care and cleaning products follow the rice, pasta, canned foods, and baking supplies, then comes the freezer aisles and bakery. Let's begin!

FRESH PRODUCE

Anything in this department is available to you as it is all fruits and vegetables. Take your time getting to know each area from the berries to the citrus, root vegetables to the leafy greens. It is recommended not to overwhelm yourself at first, so stick to what you know and every visit, pick up something you haven't tried before and given it a go. You'll find new favorite foods and ones you don't like so much, but it's all part of the fun!

- **FRUIT**
  - **Citrus fruits**: Lemons, oranges, limes, grapefruit, mandarins.
  - **Stone fruits**: Peaches, plums, nectarines, cherries, apricots
  - **Melons**: Watermelon, honeydew, cantaloupe
  - **Berries**: Strawberries, raspberries, blueberries, blackberries, gooseberries, kiwi
  - **Tropical fruits**: Banana, mango, pineapple, papaya, dragon fruit, lychee, coconut, passionfruit
  - **Apples and pears**: Granny Smith, Braeburn, golden delicious, red delicious, pink lady, gala, Fuji, McIntosh.

- **Dates and figs**: you will find fresh in the produce aisle.

- **VEGETABLES**
  - **Roots**: Potato, sweet potato, yam, carrot, beets, celeriac, radish, parsnip, ginger, turmeric, turnip.
  - **Bulbs**: Garlic, onion, shallots, green onion.
  - **Stems**: Celery, asparagus, rhubarb.
  - **Marrows**: Pumpkin, acorn squash, spaghetti squash, gem squash.
  - **Cruciferous**: Broccoli, cauliflower, Brussel sprouts, cabbage.
  - **Leafy greens**: Lettuce, spinach, collard greens, chard, arugula, kale, bok choy, watercress.
  - **Peppers**: Bell, chili, jalapeno, habanero, banana pepper.
  - **Other**: Mushrooms, cucumber, zucchini, eggplant, tomato, cherry tomato artichoke, avocado, beans, peas, corn, sprouts.

- **FRESH HERBS:**
  - **Leafy herbs**: Basil, cilantro, parsley, mint.
  - **Cooking herbs**: Marjoram, oregano, sage, thyme, rosemary, anise, caraway, bay leaves, kefir lime leaves.

- Accompaniment herbs: Dill, chives, fennel, lavender.

DRIED FOODS

These foods are mainly fruits, herbs, and spices and also apply to the bulk bin sections, which are a great way to try new foods and flavors without paying much money or worrying that you'll be stuck with a huge amount of something you won't like.

- **Nuts:** Almonds, brazil nuts, cashews, hazelnuts, macadamias, pecans, pistachios, pine nuts, walnuts.
- **Seeds:** Chia seeds, flax seeds, flaxseed meal, hemp hearts, sesame seeds, sunflower seeds, pumpkin seeds, hemp hearts.
- **Dried Fruit:** Apricots, dates, figs, mulberries, cranberries, raisins, blueberries, banana chips, mango, goji berries, shredded coconut, desiccated coconut.
- **Dried Herbs:** Basil, celery seed, cloves, coriander seeds, dill, Italian herbs, oregano, parsley, rosemary, sage, thyme.
- **Dried Spices:** Black pepper, cardamom, chili powder, chili flakes, cinnamon, cumin, curry powder, garlic powder, nutmeg, onion powder, paprika, turmeric.
- **Salt:** Sea salt, pink Himalayan salt, black salt.

- **Dried legumes:** Black beans, chickpeas, red kidney beans, white kidney beans, pinto beans, lentils, cannellini beans.
- **Other:** Nutritional yeast, kelp flakes, dried seaweed, nori sheets, rice paper rounds.

CANNED FOODS

This aisle is a haven for a vegan with so many whole food options that can be kept in a pantry for emergencies, additions to meals and has a very long shelf life. Obviously fresh foods are better for you but rotating canned foods into your diet will help ensure you have enough options to keep you happy on this new lifestyle. The following is a recommended list of handy and delicious items that work well in recipes. If you have a favorite canned vegetable or fruit that is not on this list, please continue to enjoy it.

- **Vegetables:** Diced/chopped tomatoes, tomato puree, corn, pumpkin puree, beets.
- **Fruits:** Coconut milk, coconut cream, peaches, pears, pineapple, apples, jackfruit.
- **Legumes:** Black beans, lentils, red kidney beans, white kidney beans, pinto beans, chickpeas, cannellini beans, butter beans, bean salad, vegan refried beans (caution as a lot of refried beans contain pork lard)

JAR GOODS:

Often better than canned goods due to being stored in glass rather than tin. There are many amazing food items in this area that should be kept and savored in your fridge or pantry. They are often richer in flavor than their fresh counterparts and marinated in herbs, spices, and oils that complement meals very well.

- **Vegetables:** Olives, sundried tomatoes, pickles, banana peppers, roasted red peppers, salsa, sauerkraut, capers, artichoke hearts.
- **Fruit:** Applesauce, high-quality whole jams or spreads.

NUT AND SEED BUTTERS

You won't be sorry you found this aisle. These butters are full of concentrated proteins, fibers, and vitamins and are essential to recipes at any meal of the day from smoothies to satays to desserts.

- **Nut Butters:** Almond butter, cashew butter, hazelnut butter, peanut butter, peanut and coconut butter, macadamia butter, walnut butter.
- **Seed Butters:** Pumpkin seed butter, sunflower seed butter, tahini.

GRAINS

Grains can be found in multiple areas of the grocery store. The cheaper items can be found in the bulk section, the higher priced items will be found in the health food aisle and they can also be found in the baking aisle. It is recommended that you take your time finding the brands and types that work for you, but if you are trying something for the first time, start in the bulk section.

- **Rice:** White rice, brown rice, wild rice, basmati rice, jasmine rice, long grain rice, short grain rice, saffron rice.
- **Pasta:** Linguine, spaghetti, penne, macaroni, lasagna, cannelloni, shell pasta. (most of these can be found in whole wheat varieties to up the nutrient factor and there are also very good gluten-free pasta brands now too)
- **Oats**: Rolled oats, quick oats, steel-cut oats.
- **Grains:** Amaranth, bulgur wheat, barley, couscous, quinoa, buckwheat, millet.
- **Other:** Popcorn.

BAKING AND COOKING

There are many items in this aisle that are essential to creating dishes to help you recreate favorite meals from before this transition. There are also a lot of processed and refined items that are damaging to your health. Do your best to choose the whole-grain, raw and whole varieties as much as possible.

- **Flour:** All-purpose, almond, buckwheat, chickpea, coconut, whole wheat, rice flour.

- **Baking:** Arrowroot powder, tapioca starch, potato starch, corn starch, baking powder, baking soda, agar-agar, cocoa powder, cacao powder.
- **Sugar:** Raw sugar, brown sugar, coconut sugar, blackstrap molasses.
- **Sweeteners:** Maple syrup, agave syrup, stevia.
- **Other:** Vegan chocolate chips, vegan cooking chocolate, cacao nibs, vanilla extract.

SAUCES, OILS, AND CONDIMENTS

One of the most important aisles for cooking vegan meals. There are many ethnic and cultural items that you may have never heard of before but are packed with flavor. Be cautious of fish sauce or seafood ingredients in Asian sauces and flavorings.

- **Vinegars**: Balsamic vinegar, red wine vinegar, white wine vinegar, rice wine vinegar, apple cider vinegar, malt vinegar.
- **Oils:** Avocado oil, olive oil, coconut oil, sesame oil, peanut oil, sunflower oil, hemp oil, flax oil, walnut oil, canola oil, coconut cooking spray.
- **Condiments:** Ketchup, Dijon mustard, yellow mustard, whole grain mustard, vegan mayonnaise, sriracha, hot sauce, sweet chili sauce.
- **Sauces:** Soy sauce, coconut amino, tamari (gf).

- **Others:** Miso Paste

FREEZER SECTION

A great place to find staple items that come in very handy when you've run out of fresh produce or want to keep something fresh that you use often.

- **Vegetables:** Mixed, peas, carrots, corn, spinach, broccoli, cauliflower rice, avocado
- **Fruit:** Mixed berries, blueberries, raspberries, strawberries, blackberries, smoothie mix, mango, banana, cranberries, cherries.
- **Meat Substitutes:** Vegan mince, vegan burger patties, vegan chicken filets.
- **Other:** Phyllo pastry, puff pastry (just check the ingredients for oil instead of butter)

CHILLED SECTION

Some supermarkets keep the vegan items next to the dairy items, whereas other supermarkets will keep the vegan fridges next to the fresh produce. Take your time getting acquainted with your own supermarket.

- **Milk:** Almond milk, coconut milk, cashew milk, rice milk, oat milk, hemp milk, soymilk.

- **Cheese:** Vegan sour cream, vegan cream cheese.
  There are many great vegan kinds of cheese out there ranging from soy cheese to nut cheese. There is also a great variety of types from shredded, blocks, creams, and slices.
- **Yogurt:** Coconut yogurt, almond yogurt, soy yogurt, cashew yogurt.
- **Butter:** Vegan margarine (used as margarine and also for cooking and baking)
- **Meat substitutes:** Veggie burgers, breakfast patties, vegan sausages, deli slices.
- **Other:** Silky tofu, extra firm tofu, coconut water, orange juice.

BAKERY

Lots of goodies in this section that are not what you want in your cupboard or that contain dairy or eggs. If you stick to the edges of this section and avoid the cases, you should navigate yourself quite easily.

- **Bread:** Sourdough loaf, rye bread, multigrain bread, unsliced bakery loaf, baguettes, bagels, English muffins. (some bread contains egg or milk so check the labels)
- **Wraps:** Large tortilla, mini tortillas, corn tortillas.

OTHER:

Extras that are usually found in the health food aisle.

- Vegan protein powder
- Vegan protein bars
- Spirulina
- Greens powder

TIPS AND TRICKS AT THE GROCERY STORE:

The number one hardest thing about going vegan can be a sense of loss. We are creatures of habit and we get used to having the things we like, so when these things are taken away and not replaced with something else, the sense of grief will derail our commitments and see us reaching for what we promised ourselves we would give up.

So, how do we avoid this from happening when going vegan? You've already accomplished the first part which is educating ourselves on why we are giving up the meat, dairy and eggs and positive reasons for how doing so will improve our lives.

The second part is to make sure we don't feel like we've given anything up. The best way to do this is by taking a hard look at your previous diet. Write down what your favorite meals are, what you would take for lunch, what you would have for breakfast every day, and most importantly, what were your favorite treats. Once you have this written down, try to find reasons as to why you have chosen these foods and meals. Is it because they taste good? Or remind you of something? Do they make you feel a certain way when you're done? Full, or satisfied, energized or guilty? Once you've figured this part out, you might begin to understand your relationship with food a little better.

Now, we need to find vegan replacements for these meals and food items that will replicate these feelings, so you never feel like you're missing out.

For example:

- o You usually have a fried egg and white toast with butter for breakfast because it's quick to make and fills you up and is simple. You might really enjoy switching to avocado toast instead. The avocado will mimic the egg and butter in fat content, and a sprinkle of hemp or chia seeds on top will help to replace the protein from the egg. You could switch your white toast for a good quality whole wheat toast that will keep you fuller for longer but still takes the same amount of time to make. A sprinkle of nutritional yeast will and sea salt with black pepper will keep it tasty and you happy.
- o You only eat tuna salad sandwiches for lunch with a packet of chips. Switch the tuna salad for a chickpea salad that you can make ahead of time. Make sure you have a delicious soft whole wheat bread or bun to satisfy the carb side of this equation. Find a good quality root vegetable chip to tide you over while you slowly switch this to a nut and seed snack mix and maybe some sliced veggie sticks.

- Your afternoon snack is always yogurt and chocolate biscuits. There are fantastic coconut or almond yogurts out there now! Try a few to find a good replacement that has a similar taste to your old favorite. Maybe trade your chocolate biscuit for a trail mix that has some pretzels and vegan chocolate chips in there.
- You adore chips and dip and can't imagine giving that up at night while you watch TV. Okay! Maybe keep the chips for now but sub the dip for homemade guacamole or hummus. Slowly incorporate veggie sticks and delicious seed crackers into the mix as you slowly pull the chips out of your nighttime routine.

As you can see, there are so many ways to trick yourself into a new diet and lifestyle. Please just be patient with yourself, love yourself for trying to be healthier, and keep reminding yourself of all the good that is about to come your way with this new way of being.

Chapter 6: Smoothie Recipes

Smoothies are the best way to get an excellent combination of nutrients into a small and delicious parcel. They are easy to make and are great at hiding not so tasty ingredients into a delicious treat. The following recipes range from deliciously decadent to energy inducing to micronutrient powerhouse! Enjoy!

For all the following recipes, the temperature of your smoothie is up to you. Some people like them very icy, while others prefer them just chilled. In order to cater these to your preference, some ingredients will be listed as fresh or frozen. This means that either way works great, but the frozen ones will obviously make the drink much colder. If, however, you really like icy smoothies but only have fresh ingredients, then add some ice cubes before blending to create the temperature you desire.

One other note is to gauge how long your smoothie will be kept before consumption. If you are blending a smoothie in the morning to take to work for your afternoon snack, then it is recommended to make it very icy to keep the ingredients fresh and whole for when you get around to enjoying it.

BREAKFAST SMOOTHIES – The ultimate start to the day comes in a cup. These smoothies are packed with protein, complex carbohydrates, nutrients, and healthy fats to give you the best start to the day possible.

Banana Oat

- Banana (one medium fresh or frozen)
- Rolled oats (half cup)
- Flaxseed meal (two tablespoons)
- Hemp hearts (two tablespoons)
- Vanilla extract (half teaspoon)
- Salt (tiniest pinch)
- Cinnamon (quarter teaspoon)
- Maple syrup (one teaspoon)
- Oat milk (one and a half cups)

Nutter Butter

- Rolled oats (quarter cup)
- Almond butter (one tablespoon)
- Hemp hearts (one tablespoon)

- Cinnamon (half teaspoon)
- Maple syrup (two teaspoons)
- Banana (one medium fresh or frozen)
- Salt (small pinch)
- Almond milk (one and quarter cups)

Blueberry Knockout

- Kale (one and a half cups packed fresh leaves)
- Spirulina powder (one teaspoon)
- Avocado (half one medium)
- Vanilla protein powder (one scoop)
- Maple syrup (one tablespoon)
- Blueberries (one cup fresh or frozen)
- Almond milk (one and a half cups)

Berry Blast

- Strawberries (half cup fresh or frozen)
- Raspberries (half cup fresh or frozen)
- Blackberries (half cup fresh or frozen)
- Chia seeds (two tablespoons)
- Ground cardamom (half teaspoon)
- Medjool dates (two medium fresh or dried)
- Almond milk (one and quarter cups)

Mocha Delight

- Instant espresso powder (three teaspoons)
- Cocoa powder (three teaspoons)
- Medjool dates (three medium fresh or dried)
- Hemp hearts (two tablespoons)
- Banana (one medium)
- Oat milk (one cup)

Banana Spice
- Almond butter (three teaspoons)
- Banana (one medium)
- Medjool dates (two medium fresh or dried)
- Cinnamon (quarter teaspoon)
- Ground ginger (quarter teaspoon)
- Oat milk (one cup)

TROPICAL SMOOTHIES – Summer days filled with citrus, tropical fruits and coconut. For the days when you just want to be taken away to another place.

Hawaiian Vacation
- Fresh lime juice (half one lime)
- Fresh whole ginger (thumbnail sized piece)
- Banana (1 whole fresh or frozen)
- Mango (half cup diced fresh or frozen)
- Pineapple (half cup diced fresh or frozen)

- Coconut milk (one cup)

Pina Co-Lala

- Banana (one medium)
- Pineapple (one cup diced/crushed fresh or frozen)
- Hemp hearts (two tablespoons)
- Coconut milk (one cup)

Coconut fields

- Pineapple (half cup fresh or frozen)
- Mango (half cup fresh or frozen)
- Shredded coconut (two tablespoons)
- Flaxseed meal (one tablespoon)
- Banana (one medium fresh or frozen)
- Spinach (one cup fresh leaves)
- Coconut oil (one tablespoon)
- Mint (half cup fresh leaves)
- Coconut milk (one and a half cups)

Tropical Sunset

- Coconut oil (two teaspoons)
- Coconut milk (one cup)
- Strawberries (half cup diced fresh or frozen)
- Mango (half cup diced fresh or frozen)

POWER SMOOTHIES – A great way to incorporate extra protein or organ support into your day. These smoothies are delicious but pack a powerful nutrient punch.

Almond Amazon

- Banana (one medium fresh or frozen)
- Vanilla protein powder (one scoop)
- Almond butter (two tablespoons)
- Medjool dates (two fresh or dried)
- Flaxseed meal (one tablespoon)
- Almond milk (one cup)

Golden Warrior

- Spinach (half cup fresh leaves)
- Avocado (half medium)
- Strawberries (half cup fresh or frozen)
- Walnuts (quarter cup)
- Blueberries (half cup fresh or frozen)
- Banana (one medium)
- Hemp hearts (one tablespoon)
- Ground turmeric (one teaspoon)
- Almond milk (one and a half cups)

Blood Builder

- Kale (half cup fresh leaves)

- Strawberries (half cup fresh or frozen)
- Spinach (half cup fresh or frozen)
- Beets (half cup grated fresh)
- Banana (one medium fresh or frozen)
- Cocoa powder (one tablespoon)
- Orange juice (one cup)
- Coconut milk (half cup)

DECADENT SMOOTHIES – For the times you need something extra to get you through your day. These smoothies are loaded with ingredients to keep you going but also satisfy that sweet tooth.

Apple Pie
- Almond butter (three teaspoons)
- Apple (one medium peeled, cored and diced)
- Vanilla essence (one teaspoon)
- Medjool dates (two medium)
- Cinnamon (half teaspoon)
- Nutmeg (quarter teaspoon)
- Cardamom (quarter teaspoon)
- Almond milk (one and quarter cups)

Cherry Delicious
- Almond butter (three teaspoons)

- Banana (half one medium)
- Vanilla extract (one teaspoon)
- Cherries (one cup fresh or frozen)
- Almond milk (one cup)

Pumpkin Spice

- Pumpkin puree (half cup)
- Ground nutmeg (pinch)
- Cinnamon (quarter teaspoon)
- Maple syrup (one tablespoon)
- Banana (one medium fresh or frozen)
- Vanilla extract (half teaspoon)
- Vanilla protein powder (one scoop)
- Almond milk (one cup)

Parisian mornings

- Blueberries (one cup fresh or frozen)
- Lavender (one teaspoon dried or one tablespoon fresh)
- Banana (one medium fresh or frozen)
- Chia seeds (one tablespoon)
- Hemp hearts (one tablespoon)
- Almond milk (one cup)

Chocolate Peanut Butter Cup

- Banana (one medium)

- Hemp hearts (two tablespoons)
- Cocoa (one tablespoon)
- Peanut butter (two tablespoons)
- Medjool dates (two fresh or dried)
- Almond milk (one cup)

GREEN SMOOTHIES

Healthy, zesty and the tastiest way to get your green nutrients into your day.

Green Dream
- Fresh lemon juice (one whole small lemon)
- Avocado (half one medium)
- Fresh spinach (two cups)
- Cucumber (one cup diced)
- Almond milk (one cup)

Grasshopper
- Spinach (one cup fresh leaves)
- Parsley (quarter cup fresh leaves)
- Mint (quarter cup fresh leaves)
- Avocado (half one diced)
- Granny Smith apple (one medium skinned, cored and diced)
- Pineapple (half cup fresh or frozen)

- Lemon juice (half medium lemon)
- Coconut water (one and a half cups)

Green Dragon

- Cashew butter (one tablespoon)
- Hemp hearts (two tablespoons)
- Dates (two pitted)
- Banana (one and a half)
- Spinach (one cup)
- Baby kale (half cup)
- Almond milk (one cup)

Chapter 7: Breakfast Recipes

BREAKFAST ON THE GO – We all have those mornings where we don't have time to sit and enjoy much less make good decisions! This is where the drive-thru curse ruins your healthy day. Try these breakfast ideas instead to keep you sustained, healthy and happy.

Berry Breakfast Bars

These bars are so good! Make them on the weekend when you have time and you can keep them in the fridge to grab throughout the week or keep in the freezer for the rare running-late emergency. This recipe takes only thirty-five minute to make and provides for nine servings.

INGREDIENTS:

- Rolled oats (one and a half cups)

- Applesauce (half cup)
- Flaxseed meal (one tablespoon)
- Almond flour (two cups)
- Salt (quarter teaspoon)
- Blackstrap molasses (quarter cup)
- Baking powder (half teaspoon)
- Vanilla extract (one teaspoon)
- Almond butter (quarter cup)
- Apple cider vinegar (one teaspoon)
- Oat milk (half cup)
- Maple syrup (quarter cup)
- Agar agar (one tablespoon)
- Mixed frozen berries (three cups)
- Lemon juice (one teaspoon)

INSTRUCTIONS:

1. You'll need an oven-safe dish, preferably a baking dish. Square is better to get nine full-portioned squares from it, but any shape will do. Your oven should be heated to 350F and your baking dish should be lined with baking paper.

2. Mix together the oat milk, applesauce, molasses, vanilla, and almond butter. Add the almond flour and flaxseed meal and mix. If it looks too thick at this point, add a little water (maybe a tablespoon or two) to ensure it is

runny enough to accept the oats. Stir in the oats and baking powder then add the salt and mix really well to get a nice thick batter.

3. Spoon all but about one cup of mixture into the bottom of your dish and press it down with your fingers to get an even base and bake for fifteen minutes.

4. While this is in the oven, get a saucepan and over medium-high heat, cook down the frozen berries and agar-agar with half a cup of cold water. Keep an eye on it and once it comes to a boil, you should turn down the heat to medium-low and let it simmer for around five minutes while stirring as it thickens. Then take it off the heat and add the lemon juice and maple syrup, stir again and then leave to thicken.

5. Pour this over the oat base and with your fingers, roughly crumble the cup of oat mixture you put aside over the top of the berry filling.

6. Put the baking dish back in the oven for another twelve minutes then take out. The oat mixture on top should be beautifully browned. Allow it to cool before you put it in the fridge to set for an hour or so.

7. Cut into squares or bars or whatever makes you happy. Then wrap individually in baking paper or cling film and keep in the fridge or freezer!

Healthy Chocolate Raspberry Chia Pudding

This can be made the night before for a perfect grab-and-go situation. The chocolate and raspberry combination makes you think you're eating dessert, while the chia seeds are a great source of soluble fiber that will keep you sustained through your morning. This recipe provides for two servings, and you can make it on a Sunday to keep in your fridge for the two days that you know you'll be running late in the coming week. It takes just five minutes to make but needs to set overnight.

INGREDIENTS:

- Chia seeds (half cup)
- Coconut milk (one and a half cups)
- Vanilla extract (half teaspoon)
- Frozen raspberries (half cup)
- Salt (tiny pinch)
- Maple syrup (two tablespoons)
- Cocoa powder (two tablespoons)
- Almond slivers (two tablespoons)

INSTRUCTIONS:

1. In a blender, combine raspberries, coconut milk, vanilla, salt, maple syrup, and cocoa powder. Blend until combined and smooth.

2. Pour into a bowl and add the chia seeds, then whisk to mix through.

3. Pour into two mason jars or containers, put on the lids then leave in the fridge overnight.

4. In the morning, sprinkle with almond slivers for a little crunch and fresh sliced bananas or raspberries if you wish.

5. Don't forget to bring a spoon with you! Enjoy.

LIGHT BREAKFASTS – For the mornings when you don't want a heavy breakfast or don't have much time to prepare or eat a meal.

Ultimate Avocado Toast

This recipe is quick and easy to make and delicious. No cooking is required, it is simply piling these flavorful whole foods on top of your favorite toast! This provides enough for one hungry person or two not-so-hungry people. Feel free to omit or add any ingredients to appeal to your tastes.

INGREDIENTS:

- Your favorite vegan bread (two slices)
- Basil (three fresh leaves)
- Salt (a generous pinch)

- Cherry tomato (four small tomatoes)
- Hemp hearts (one teaspoon)
- Avocado (one medium ripe)
- Sesame seeds (half teaspoon)
- Nutritional yeast (half teaspoon)
- Red onion (one teaspoon diced)
- Black pepper (a generous pinch)
- Lemon juice (one teaspoon)

INSTRUCTIONS:

1. Mash avocado with lemon juice.
2. Toast bread to your liking (more well done is better).
3. Spread avocado generously on toast.
4. Mix together black pepper, hemp hearts, sesame seeds, and nutritional yeast until seeds are coated.
5. Salt avocado then sprinkle seed mix on top.
6. Slice cherry tomatoes and basil. Sprinkle over toast along with the diced red onion.

Tofu Scramble

A great dupe for real scrambled eggs! This recipe is easy to make and makes enough for two people. Enjoy with toast or veggies for a quick and delicious breakfast. It takes fifteen minutes to prepare.

INGREDIENTS:

- Firm tofu (one standard pack)
- Curry powder (one teaspoon)
- Turmeric powder (quarter teaspoon)
- Black salt aka Kala namak (one teaspoon)
- Canola oil (one teaspoon)

INSTRUCTIONS:

1. Break up the tofu into a crumbly/chunky consistency.
2. Add to a hot and oiled fry pan and follow with curry, turmeric and black salt.
3. Stir over high heat until desired texture is reached. (6 minutes for the soft scramble and 12 minutes for a crispy version)
4. Enjoy with your favorite toast

Christmas Granola

This recipe smells and tastes like the holidays but can be enjoyed all year round! It can be made ahead of time, takes only fifteen minutes and makes enough for at least five portions, so make it on Sunday to get you through the coming work week!

INGREDIENTS:

- Rolled oats (six cups)

- Maple syrup (one cup)
- Coconut oil (three-quarter cup)
- Hemp hearts (three tablespoons)
- Pecans (quarter cup)
- Nutmeg (one teaspoon)
- Ground ginger (two teaspoons)
- Cinnamon (two tablespoons)

INSTRUCTIONS:

1. Put everything into a big bowl and mix, mix, mix until you get a chunky mixture.
2. Divide the mixture onto two baking trays and press it out to cover.
3. Put it in the oven on 360F and bake for seven minutes before switching oven shelves so they bake evenly for a further five or so minutes. They should be a beautiful brown in color and smell amazing.
4. Take it out and let it cool off, then break it up by poking with the wrong end of a wooden spoon and put it into an airtight container.
5. Enjoy it with your favorite dairy-free milk and fresh fruit!

OATMEAL – Quick, filling, delicious and substantial. Oatmeal is a slow-burning meal that maintains energy

levels throughout the morning. Overnight oats can be prepared the night before to save time in the morning.

Warm Blueberry Over-night Oats

Not as quick as regular overnight oats as this requires a little heating in the morning, but you get a syrupy, berry-filled meal that is warm, satisfying and delicious. This recipe takes around fifteen minutes to make and provides one serving.

INGREDIENTS:

- Frozen blueberries (half cup)
- Fresh blueberries (quarter cup)
- Vanilla extract (quarter teaspoon)
- Shredded coconut (half teaspoon)
- Maple syrup (one teaspoon)
- Almond milk (three-quarter cup)
- Rolled oats (three-quarter cup)

INSTRUCTIONS:

1. Put oats and almond milk into mason jar or container and leave in the fridge overnight.
2. In the morning, on medium heat, put syrup, vanilla extract and frozen blueberries into a saucepan. Heat until blueberries have cooked through and the mixture has become sauce-like.

3. Spoon the overnight oats into the saucepan and gently fold it through the blueberry sauce. Once the oats are warmed through then put the oats into a bowl and top with a little more almond milk if you desire, then the fresh blueberries and coconut.

Chocolate Raspberry Overnight Oats

How can you possibly resist? If you have trouble eating healthy breakfasts because all you want is donuts and treats, then this recipe could be the answer you've been looking for. Sweet, delicious, healthy and nutritious. The best of all worlds. This takes five minutes to prepare and is enough for one person.

INGREDIENTS
- Almond butter (one teaspoon)
- Cocoa powder (one tablespoon)
- Maple syrup (one teaspoon)
- Almond milk (three-quarter cup)
- Frozen raspberries (quarter cup)
- Cacao nibs (two tablespoons)

INSTRUCTIONS:
1. In a mason jar or heat-safe glass container, put all ingredients together and give it a generous stir or shake (with the lid on of course).
2. Put it in the fridge over-night.

3. In the morning, take out of the fridge, give it a good stir and enjoy in the way you like best by reading the extra notes below:

    a. If you like cold oatmeal, then do nothing!

    b. You can add a little more almond milk if you find it too thick.

    c. If you don't like cold oatmeal, you can put the jar/container with the lid off into a saucepan and pour cold water around the jar/container and slowly heat over medium-low heat. It is important to put the jar into cold water so the jar can heat slowly with the cold water to prevent any breakages and ruined oatmeal. The oatmeal will warm slowly while you go about your morning routine and you can enjoy beautifully warm oatmeal after ten to fifteen minutes.

Loaded Oatmeal

For those who just adore oatmeal with the works that sticks to your ribs. This is the recipe for you. It takes only ten minutes to make and provides for two people!

INGREDIENTS:

- Flaxseed meal (two tablespoons)
- Peanut butter (two tablespoons)
- Coconut (two tablespoons desiccated)

- Banana (one medium)
- Nutmeg (a generous pinch)
- Cinnamon (half teaspoon)
- Vanilla extract (half teaspoon)
- Salt (a generous pinch)
- Maple syrup (two tablespoons)
- Oat milk (one cup)
- Rolled oats (one cup)

INSTRUCTIONS:

1. In a saucepan over medium-high heat, put oat milk and oats with one cup of water and bring to a boil.
2. Reduce to medium-low and add syrup, vanilla, nutmeg, salt, and cinnamon, and stir until the oatmeal is the consistency that appeals most to you.
3. Before you take it out of the saucepan, add the peanut butter and flaxseed meal and stir through.
4. Divide into two bowls and sprinkle with the coconut and top with sliced banana. Enjoy!

CLASSIC BREAKFASTS – Great substitute breakfasts for old favorites so you don't feel so out of place when cooking for or eating with your non-vegan friends!

Tofu Breakfast Burrito

This burrito is a decadent feast for a hungry vegan! It takes around twenty minutes to prepare and will serve one person a beautiful Mexican breakfast meal!

INGREDIENTS

- Whole wheat quesadilla (one large)
- Jalapeno (one small)
- Red bell pepper (half one medium)
- Red onion (half one medium)
- Corn (half cup)
- Avocado (half one medium)
- Tomatoes (two medium)
- Cilantro (half cup)
- Garlic (three cloves)
- Lime juice (one medium lime)
- Black salt (half teaspoon)
- Nutritional yeast (two tablespoons)
- Firm tofu (one package)
- Canola oil (one tablespoon)

INSTRUCTIONS:

1. First, make pico de gallo in a small bowl. Cut open the tomatoes and scoop out and discard of the seeds and pulp then finely dice the firm flesh. Add one clove of garlic, a quarter of one red onion, half of one jalapeno

all finely diced. Chop a quarter cup of cilantro, add to the bowl and then top with the juice of half one lime. Mix together and set aside.

2. Heat oil in a frying pan over medium heat and add a quarter of one red onion, the bell pepper and half of one jalapeno all diced. Cook until the vegetables are soft then add two cloves of garlic finely diced.

3. In another pan on low heat, heat the tortilla by first lightly rubbing with a little oil (drizzle a tiny amount on one side of the tortilla then gently rub over the surface with clean fingers and put into the pan oiled side down).

4. Add the broken-up tofu (just crumble by hand into the pan), along with the nutritional yeast, corn, salt and the juice of half one lime. Cook until well-combined and heated through.

5. Put a tortilla on a plate crispy side down and scoop the tofu scramble into the center of it. Spoon pico de gallo on top of the tofu followed by diced fresh avocado. Fold the edges of the tortilla over the filling and then roll to make a burrito. Enjoy!

Classic French Toast

The dish enjoyed around the world can also be enjoyed by a vegan! This recipe is easy to prepare and is a good source of fiber thanks to the addition of the flaxseed meal. It will provide for two people and takes around twenty minutes to prepare.

INGREDIENTS:
- Vegan brioche loaf (half a regular loaf)
- Oat milk (one cup)
- Salt (a generous pinch)
- Cinnamon (one teaspoon)
- Vanilla extract (one teaspoon)
- Nutmeg (quarter teaspoon)
- Flaxseed meal (two tablespoons)

INSTRUCTIONS:
1. Slice six one-inch pieces of bread from a loaf.
2. Whisk together milk and flaxseed and set aside for three minutes.
3. Add vanilla, cinnamon, salt, and nutmeg and whisk again.
4. Oil and heat a frying pan on medium.
5. Dunk bread slices into the mixture until coated and fry for 3-5 minutes until a desirable color texture.
6. Top French toast with sliced strawberries and maple syrup.

Banana French Toast

This decadent and filling French toast version is sure to impress your guests. It is packed with flavor and sweetness and tastes like it was prepared by a chef. It provides for two people.

INGREDIENTS:

- Vegan sourdough loaf (half a regular loaf)
- Banana (three medium ripe)
- Brown sugar (two tablespoons)
- Flour (two tablespoons)
- Almond milk (half cup and two tablespoons)
- Cinnamon (three-quarter teaspoon)
- Nutmeg (quarter teaspoon)
- Salt (a generous pinch)
- Black pepper (small pinch)
- Vanilla extract (half teaspoon)
- Coconut oil (one teaspoon)
- Maple syrup (two tablespoons)

INSTRUCTIONS:

1. Cut bread into six one-inch slices.
2. Blend one banana with half cup milk, syrup, flour, vanilla, oil, half teaspoon cinnamon, salt, and pepper.
3. Heat a saucepan over medium and add two sliced bananas, brown sugar, two tablespoons milk and quarter teaspoon cinnamon. Stir while on heat mixture

caramelizes, remove from heat once a dark golden-brown color and syrupy in texture

4. Oil and heat a frying pan over medium.

5. Dunk bread slices into the mixture until coated and cook for five minutes each side until it becomes easy to move around the pan and is dark brown in color.

6. Top French toast slices with caramelized banana syrup and maple syrup.

Mega Vegan Breakfast Sandwich

Just because you're vegan, does not mean you have to miss out on one of the best things to be invented. The breakfast sandwich is pure indulgence with egg and sausage, mayo and cheese, onion and tomato on a toasted English muffin! Let's face it, it's not the healthiest of breakfast ideas, but it's just so tasty and satisfying! Well, this recipe doesn't fall far from this tree – it's not the healthiest, but a LOT healthier than its original version, and it IS tasty! It takes 40 minutes to prepare but provides for four people!

INGREDIENTS:

- English muffins (four muffins)
- Firm tofu (quarter cup crumbled)
- Turmeric powder (a generous pinch)
- Paprika (one teaspoon)
- Chickpea flour (two tablespoons)
- Tapioca starch (two tablespoons)

- Black salt (quarter teaspoon)
- Regular salt (half teaspoon)
- Onion powder (quarter teaspoon)
- Garlic powder (half teaspoon)
- Tomato (one medium)
- Canola oil (two teaspoons)
- Nutritional yeast (three tablespoons)
- Oat milk (quarter cup)
- Coconut milk (three-quarter cup)
- Red onion (quarter one medium)
- Apple cider vinegar (one teaspoon)
- Green onions (two sprigs)
- Black pepper (four pinches)
- Vegan breakfast patties (pack of four)

INSTRUCTIONS:

1. First, we make our cheese! In a saucepan, put coconut milk, quarter teaspoon paprika, garlic powder, regular salt, nutritional yeast, and tapioca starch. Bring it to a boil while stirring, then quickly reduce the heat to medium-low and continue to stir for another minute until it gets a little stretchy. Once this happens, set it aside.

2. Next, we make our egg. In a blender, put tofu, oat milk, chickpea flour, three quarter teaspoons paprika, apple cider vinegar, onion powder, turmeric, black salt, and

canola oil. Blend until a similar consistency to pancake batter. If it's too thick, add more oat milk, if it's too watery, add a little more chickpea flour.

3. Heat and oil a frypan over medium, and spoon in the mixture into portions that are just bigger than your English muffins. Cook until it starts to dry out on top, then flip and cook for another two minutes then keep to the side.

4. In the same fry pan and with a little more oil, cook up the vegan breakfast patties following the instructions on the packet then set aside.

5. Toast the muffins and put four pieces on a board. Put a breakfast patty on each muffin, then top with a small teaspoon of your stretchy cheese sauce. Add a vegan egg and then another little teaspoon of cheese sauce. Top this with red onion and tomato slices, then a little more cheese sauce, then sprinkle with finely chopped green onion and black pepper and finally the other half of the English muffin.

6. Enjoy your breakfast sandwich feast!

SUNDAY BRUNCH – The meal that requires decadence, indulgence and sharing. These recipes are sure to deliver on all levels.

The Farmers Vegan Breakfast

You don't have to for-go this full traditional breakfast! Soft and fluffy scrambled eggs, breakfast patties, potato hash, sautéed tomato and mushrooms and toast with avocado. This meal is big and hearty and made to enjoy on a slow Sunday morning with friends and family. It takes around thirty minutes to prepare and will serve three people.

INGREDIENTS:
- Pinto beans (one can)
- Olive oil (three tablespoons)
- Garlic (three cloves)
- Oat flour (three tablespoons)
- Chili flakes (quarter teaspoon)
- Maple syrup (one tablespoon)
- Portobello mushrooms (three medium)
- Soy sauce (two teaspoons)
- Fresh parsley (two sprigs)
- Onion powder (two teaspoons)
- Garlic powder (two teaspoons)
- Dried thyme (quarter teaspoon)
- Tomatoes (three medium)
- Avocado (one and one half)
- Paprika (two teaspoons)
- Salt and pepper (to season as you go)
- Baby spinach (two cups packed)

- Dried rosemary (a half teaspoon or quarter teaspoon fresh)
- Dried sage (one teaspoon)
- Balsamic vinegar (one tablespoon)
- Potatoes (two medium)
- White onion (three quarters one medium)
- Thick cut sourdough bread (six slices)

INSTRUCTIONS:

1. First, we'll make our potatoes! Wash your potatoes then grate them into a bowl with a cheese grater. Follow by a grating quarter of a white onion. With clean hands, roughly combine and then pick up a handful of time and squeeze as much liquid out as possible before putting on a clean kitchen towel. Continue until the entire mixture is on the towel, then gather it up and squeeze the remaining liquid out and put it back into the liquid-free bowl.

2. Drizzle one tablespoon of olive oil over the mixture and top with one teaspoon of paprika and enough salt and pepper to satisfy your taste preference. Mix through with your hands until the oil and spices are very thoroughly combined with the potato and onion.

3. Divide into three portions and place on a baking tray with baking paper and press out until they are about one cm thick.

4. Put into the oven at 475F on the highest shelf and bake for 20 minutes while we make the breakfast patties.

5. Next, the breakfast patties; drain the can of pinto beans into a bowl so you can keep the liquid. Mash the beans with a fork until they are half chunky and half mushy.

6. Then add back to it two tablespoons of the saved liquid (discard the rest), the dried sage, rosemary, thyme, onion and garlic powders, chili flakes and one teaspoon of paprika. Stir thoroughly to combine.

7. Add the oat flour, maple syrup, and soy sauce and stir again.

8. Roll this mixture into six equal balls and place on a baking tray with baking paper. Press each ball down to form a nice sized patty. It shouldn't be too thin, or it will break apart when it is cooked.

9. It should have been about twenty minutes since you put the hash in the oven and the edges should be starting to brown. Turn them over carefully with a spatula and put them back in the oven on the top shelf, then put the patties in the oven on a middle shelf and cook these for eight minutes.

10. After eight minutes, turn them over and cook for a further eight minutes, then turn off the oven and remove both the hash and the patties. Set aside.

11. Now, we will cook the mushrooms and veggies. Heat a frypan with two tablespoons of olive oil over medium-

low and add half a chopped white onion. Cook until it begins to soften.

12. Add sliced portobello mushrooms and turn the heat up to medium-high. Sprinkle the mushrooms and onions with salt and pepper to taste.

13. When the mushrooms begin to sweat down and darken, add three cloves of finely diced garlic, the spinach, and the tomatoes cut into large chunks.

14. Add more salt and pepper if it needs more seasoning, then drizzle with the balsamic vinegar and toss everything together.

15. Remove from heat once cooked to your liking and on three plates, dish out the hash browns, then two patties per plate, divide the mushroom mixture evenly and then add two slices of sourdough and top the plates with a half a sliced avocado each. Finely chop the fresh parsley and sprinkle over everything. Serve and enjoy!

Mushroom Mix Avocado Toast

This recipe is delicious, filling, healthy and substantial. Your friends will love it and so will you! It is relatively easy to prepare but tastes like it took a long time where the preparation time is merely twenty-five minutes. It provides for two people.

INGREDIENTS:

- Mushrooms (one cup sliced)
- Miso paste (one tablespoon)
- Balsamic vinegar (one tablespoon)
- White onion (two tablespoons)
- Sesame seeds (one tablespoon)
- Multigrain bread (four slices)
- Avocado (one medium ripe)
- Lemon juice (one tablespoon)
- Cannellini beans (one-third can)
- Baby kale (three-quarter cup)

INSTRUCTIONS:

1. Oil and heat a frying pan over medium.
2. Slice onions and put in the pan, add mushrooms and balsamic vinegar, cook until they begin to caramelize.
3. Stir in beans and kale and cook until kale is wilted.
4. Whisk miso paste with a little water (two teaspoons) and add to the pan.
5. Spread avocado onto toasted bread, then top with mushroom mixture and sprinkle with sesame seeds.

Breakfast Tacos

Fun and delicious, this recipe only serves one so multiply it by the number of people you're feeding, and you have a feast for the masses that is satisfying and doesn't feel like a whole-food meal.

Add vegan sour cream and salsa for dipping and drizzling if you want to make it extra authentic! This recipe takes around forty minutes to prepare.

INGREDIENTS:

- Mini tortillas (three)
- Firm tofu (quarter cup crumbled)
- Black salt (quarter teaspoon)
- Regular salt (quarter teaspoon)
- Red potato (one medium)
- Nutritional yeast (two teaspoons)
- Onion (two tablespoons diced)
- Green onion (two sprigs)
- Avocado (half one medium)
- Tomato (one small)
- Paprika (quarter teaspoon)
- Chili flakes (quarter teaspoon)
- Garlic powder (half teaspoon)
- Dried thyme (quarter teaspoon)
- Dried sage (quarter teaspoon)

INSTRUCTIONS:

1. Cube potato into dice-sized pieces and toss them with paprika, garlic powder, thyme, and sage and spread out

onto the baking sheet. Lightly drizzle with oil and sprinkle with salt and chili flakes.

2. Bake at 450F for 15 minutes, roughly toss then bake for another 15 minutes.

3. In a frypan on medium heat, drizzle in some oil and cook the onions until soft then crumble in tofu and follow with black salt and nutritional yeast. Cook until tofu is soft and heated through.

4. Place tortillas into the oven for five minutes to warm then remove and spoon onto each the scramble followed by the potatoes. Dice the green onions, avocado, and tomato and sprinkle on top of each tortilla. Fold and enjoy!

PANCAKES – The best way to enjoy a guilty pleasure is at breakfast! These vegan pancake variations are easy to make and guaranteed to impress. No one will know they're not vegan, so this is a great way to go to trick your non-vegan friends.

Blueberry Pancakes

How can you not? These are a classic and the high antioxidant profiles of blueberries make these a no-brainer – they're both delicious and nutritious. These take a good twenty minutes to prepare and they provide for two people.

INGREDIENTS:

- Blueberries (one tablespoon frozen)
- Blueberries (quarter cup fresh)
- Brown sugar (one teaspoon)
- Vanilla soymilk (three-quarter cup)
- Flour (one cup)
- Baking powder (one and a half teaspoons)
- Salt (small pinch)

INSTRUCTIONS:

1. Whisk sugar, salt, flour, and baking powder together.
2. Blend milk and frozen blueberries.
3. Mix into dry ingredients.
4. Put a frying pan on medium-low heat, apply a little oil and spoon in the pancake batter. Flip when small bubbles emerge on top and let another side cook until done.
5. Top cooked pancakes with fresh blueberries and syrup.

Vanilla Raspberry Pancakes

A beautiful take on a classic. The sweet flavor of vanilla rounds out the tartness of the raspberries to create a harmony of flavors in fluffy drool-inducing pancakes. This recipe takes twenty minutes and provides for two people.

INGREDIENTS:

- Raspberries (half cup fresh or thawed frozen)
- Vanilla extract (one teaspoon)
- Oat milk (three-quarter cup)
- Brown sugar (one teaspoon)
- Baking powder (one and a half teaspoon)
- Flour (one cup)

INSTRUCTIONS:

1. Combine flour, baking powder, and sugar.
2. Add vanilla and milk then whisk until smooth.
3. Fold in raspberries.
4. Put a frying pan on medium-low heat, apply a little oil and spoon in the pancake batter. Flip when small bubbles emerge on top and let another side cook until done.
5. Top cooked pancakes with syrup and raspberries.

Chocolate Mutter Pancakes

For all the chocolate peanut butter lovers out there, you can't go past this recipe. Full of flavor and decadence, it provides for two people and takes twenty minutes to prepare.

INGREDIENTS:

- Peanut butter (two tablespoons)
- Almond milk (three-quarter cup)

- Cocoa powder (three tablespoons)
- Coconut oil (one teaspoon)
- Baking powder (one and a half teaspoons)
- Flour (one cup)
- Salt (small pinch)
- Maple syrup (one tablespoon and one teaspoon)

INSTRUCTIONS:

1. Mix two tablespoons cocoa powder with flour, salt, and baking powder.
2. Whisk in one tablespoon maple syrup, milk, and oil.
3. Put a frying pan on medium-low heat, apply a little oil and spoon in the pancake batter. Flip when small bubbles emerge on top and let another side cook until done.
4. Separately, whisk the peanut butter with enough hot water to make it a runny consistency (about a quarter cup). Mix in one tablespoon cocoa powder and one teaspoon syrup to make a sauce.
5. When pancakes are done, stack and drizzle with peanut sauce.

WAFFLES– The ultimate treat for breakfast time. Obviously, for those that own a waffle iron, these recipes are specially made for the perfect fluffy waffles that satisfy on so many levels. If you wanted these recipes to

be extra healthy, switch the flour for oat or spelt flour for a denser and more nutritionally fulfilling feast.

Banana Bread Waffles

These are so tasty and so much better for you than standard waffles. Walnuts are a great source of protein and fiber, and bananas are high in potassium. This recipe provides for two people and takes a good twenty minutes to prepare.

INGREDIENTS:
- Flour (one cup)
- Baking powder (one teaspoon)
- Coconut oil (one teaspoon)
- Cooking spray (for waffle iron)
- Maple syrup (one teaspoon)
- Almond milk (half cup)
- Banana (one whole, fresh, ripe, mashed)
- Walnuts (three tablespoons)

INSTRUCTIONS:
1. Whisk milk, oil, syrup, and banana together.
2. Finely chop two-thirds of the walnuts and blend the rest to a fine meal.
3. Into the liquids stir in the blended walnuts, baking powder, and flour.
4. Once combined, stir in the finely chopped walnuts.

5. Spray hot waffle iron and spoon on the batter. Cook until no more steam emerges from iron.

6. Top waffles with banana slices, walnut pieces, and maple syrup.

Apple Cinnamon Waffles

Apple and cinnamon just take you back to childhood memories of home-made apple pie and carefree days. The smell that wafts up to you from this plate takes you right back to that feeling. It provides for two people and takes twenty-five minutes to prepare.

INGREDIENTS:

- Almond milk (three-quarter cup)
- Coconut oil (one tablespoon)
- White sugar (one tablespoon)
- Flour (one and one-quarter cups)
- Baking powder (two teaspoons)
- Salt (small pinch)
- Apple (one medium sliced and peeled)
- Lemon juice (one teaspoon)
- Cinnamon (three-quarter teaspoon)
- Nutmeg (quarter teaspoon)
- Maple syrup (one teaspoon)

INSTRUCTIONS:

1. Combine sliced apple with syrup, lemon juice, a half cup water, and quarter teaspoon cinnamon in a saucepan and bring to boil before simmering for 20 minutes with the lid on.
2. Remove the lid for a further 10 minutes as the mixture reduces.
3. Mix remaining cinnamon with nutmeg, flour, baking powder, salt, and sugar.
4. Combine with oil and milk to make the batter.
5. Spray hot waffle iron and spoon on the batter. Cook until edges brown.
6. Top cooked waffles with apple mixture and maple syrup.

Savory Potato Hash Waffles

When waffles and potatoes get married, these are the children they deliver. Crispy, tasty hash in the waffle iron is just so special and it delights people of all ages. This recipe provides for two to three people and takes thirty minutes to make (shredding potatoes takes some time).

INGREDIENTS:
- Paprika (half teaspoon)
- Black pepper (quarter teaspoon)
- Salt (half teaspoon)
- Parsley (two fresh sprigs)

- Avocado (half one medium)
- Coconut oil (one and a half tablespoons)
- Potatoes (one pound shredded)

INSTRUCTIONS:

1. Press shredded potato between clean kitchen towels and wring out the liquid.

2. Toss together with salt, pepper, and paprika.

3. Spray hot waffle iron and spoon on mixture being sure to pack down with the back of a spoon. Cook on highest setting until golden in color (about 7 minutes).

4. When crispy to the touch and golden in color, remove and top with chopped parsley and sliced avocado.

Chapter 8: Lunch Recipes

SOUPS – Vegan soups are some of the tastiest and hearty soups you can get. Meat and dairy often take away from the amazing flavors of fresh herbs and vegetables, but these recipes will remind you what true soup is all about.

Carrot Love Soup

This soup is dedicated to the true essence of carrots like no other. The humble carrot is often forgotten about in the flashy world of vegetables, but it is an excellent source of fiber, potassium and beta carotene! The gentle spices and creamy coconut of this soup will transport you to a new level of carrot love that you've never been before. It takes just forty-five minutes to make and provides for four people.

INGREDIENTS:

- Carrots (four and a half cups chopped)
- Peanut butter (quarter cup)
- Maple syrup (one tablespoon)
- Vegetable broth (two cups)
- Curry powder (two teaspoons)
- Mild curry paste (two tablespoons)
- Fresh ginger (one tablespoon minced)
- Turmeric powder (two teaspoons)
- Garlic (two cloves)
- Onion (one cup)
- Cilantro (half cup)
- Coconut oil (one tablespoon)
- Coconut milk (two cups)

INSTRUCTIONS:

1. Put coconut oil in a large soup pot and heat on medium before adding diced onion and cooking until softened. Then add the ginger, curry paste, and powder, ginger, and turmeric and stir to release flavors.

2. Add the carrots, coconut milk, vegetable broth, and peanut butter and bring to a boil before turning down to low heat and leaving for thirty minutes to allow the carrots to cook through.

3. Blend the soup either in a blender or food processor or with a stick blender in the pot, until the soup is creamy and smooth.
4. If you used a blender or processor, then return the soup to the pot. Bring it to a boil one last time, before taking off the heat.
5. Chop the cilantro and top each serving with a generous portion. Enjoy!

Tomato Indulgence Soup

This soup is like no other tomato soup you've tried before. The delicate flavors of basil and garlic bring out the zestiness that tomatoes often lend to other dishes. Pine nuts up to the protein factor making this soup a well-rounded meal that is bursting with nutrition and goodness. It takes an hour and a half to prepare and provides six generous portions.

INGREDIENTS:
- Tomatoes (four cups)
- Pine nuts (quarter cup)
- Chili flakes (half teaspoon)
- Lemon juice (half one medium lemon)
- Balsamic vinegar (two tablespoons)
- Olive oil (half cup)
- Vegetable stock (four cups)

- Fresh basil (two cups)
- Carrots (three large)
- Onion (one medium)
- Garlic (ten cloves)
- Salt and pepper (to taste)

INSTRUCTIONS:

1. Chop up the tomatoes, carrots, and onion into chunks and toss with quarter cup olive oil and salt and pepper.
2. Tip onto a baking tray and sprinkle eight diced cloves of garlic over before working through as you spread everything out evenly. Bake at 350F for around an hour, checking on occasion to toss if required.
3. On a smaller tray, spread out the pine nuts and place on a separate shelf in the oven to toast for ten minutes.
4. In a blender, make a rustic pesto by placing the pine nuts, basil, two cloves of garlic, lemon juice and a quarter cup of olive oil. Blend until everything is combined and you can see little flecks of green and white from the basil and pine nuts. You don't want this to be too smooth.
5. Scoop out half of this mixture and set aside.
6. When the vegetables are cooked through (the carrots should be soft), then tip all the ingredients from the baking tray (including all the juice) into the blender on

top of the remaining pesto mixture. and blend until smooth.

7. You may need to do the above step in stages depending on the size of your blender. If you have a stick blender, then just transfer the remaining pesto and vegetables into a pot and blend in there.

8. Once all the veggies are blended, put the soup into a large pot and add the vegetable stock, balsamic vinegar and chili flakes. Heat over medium and stir until everything is combined and simmering.

9. Remove from heat and add a small amount of the reserved pesto to the top of each portion. Enjoy!

Hearty Tortilla Soup

The black beans and Mexican flavors in this soup speaks to your stomach in ways that few other meals do. It is hearty, delicious, flavorful and so good for you that you will enjoy it over and over and over again. Your body will thank you every time! Digestive herbs and spices mean that you can enjoy to your hearts (or stomachs) content. It takes thirty minutes to make and provides four generous servings.

INGREDIENTS:
- Black beans (one and a half cup)
- Vegetable broth (three cups)
- Cayenne pepper (quarter teaspoon)

- Dried oregano (half teaspoon)
- Garlic (four cloves)
- Jalapeno (one medium)
- Yellow bell pepper (one large)
- White onion (one small)
- Olive oil (one tablespoon)
- Ground cumin (one teaspoon)
- Paprika (one teaspoon)
- Coriander seeds (one teaspoon)
- Cilantro (one small bunch)
- Bay leaf (one)
- Tomatoes (three medium)
- Salt and pepper (to taste)
- Tortillas (two large)

INSTRUCTIONS:

1. Heat oil in a frypan over medium heat and add diced onion, finely diced bell pepper and finely diced jalapeno with a small pinch of salt. Let them cook down for a few minutes until they soften then push them to one side of the pan and tilt so the oil drains away from them to the other side. In the oil, put the coriander seeds, cayenne, cumin, and paprika and stir in the oil until the coriander seeds begin to pop.

2. Stir everything together and add the finely diced garlic. Stir through again, then tip everything into a soup pot and increase to medium-high heat.

3. Add the vegetable broth, oregano, diced tomato, bay leaf, and black beans and bring to a boil. Stir then reduce to a simmer for a further fifteen minutes.

4. Slice tortillas into quarters, then pile up and slice into strips. Toss with olive oil and a little salt and pepper. Spread out onto baking trays and bake for fifteen minutes.

5. Remove the bay leaf from the soup and with the back of a wooden spoon press the beans against the side of the pot to break them up a little. Stir again before removing from heat and serving.

6. Top each portion with a generous amount chopped cilantro and a small handful of the tortilla strips. Enjoy!

SALADS – Remove the idea of a boring salad from your mind. These recipes are so far from boring that you'll never look back! Protein packed, fiber-rich and bursting with flavor, these salads are meals in themselves, they aren't anyone's side dish!

Vegan Cobb Power Salad

Yes, just like you, the beautiful Cobb salad can be made even more beautiful and healthy by going vegan. These ingredients combine to deliver a nutrient-rich power plate that is as varied and delicious as it is colorful. Bring it to work to have all your co-workers pepper you with questions about where you got it from because it looks just too good to be homemade. This recipe is mainly prep work, which can be done the night before for quick assembly after breakfast. Total prep time is forty minutes, but if you plan ahead, it can be thrown together in less than five. It provides for 5 servings, so if you do the prep on Sunday, you'll have lunch made for the week!

INGREDIENTS:
- Red onion (quarter medium)
- Almonds (third cup)
- Dried cranberries (third cup)
- Avocado (three medium)
- Chickpeas (one can)
- Lemon juice (one and a half lemons)
- Baby kale (four cups)
- Mesculin salad mix (four cups)
- Cherry tomatoes (two cups)
- Salt and pepper (to taste)
- Olive oil (two tablespoons)
- Corn kernels (one cup)
- Garlic (one small clove)
- Sweet potatoes (two medium)

- Hemp hearts (third cup)
- Toasted sunflower seeds (half cup)
- Tahini (half cup)

INSTRUCTIONS:

1. Peel and dice the sweet potato, toss with two teaspoons oil and generous pinches of salt and pepper. Bake on a baking tray for forty minutes, tossing halfway through.
2. Clean and rinse both baby kale and mesclun mixes. To the kale, add one tablespoon olive oil, one tablespoon lemon juice and salt and pepper to taste. Massage this mixture into the kale leaves and set aside.
3. Dice the onion and tomatoes and set aside.
4. In a blender, add the tahini, juice from one lemon, garlic, salt and pepper and two tablespoons of water and blend until smooth. Add two more tablespoons of water and blend again. It should be thick yet runny enough to drizzle.
5. Per portion, there should be one handful of kale and one handful of mesculin. Toss the correct amount together and make a bed of greens on the plate. On top of this, put little piles of all the remaining ingredients to make a patchwork of color and variety. These will include red onion, tomatoes, corn, almonds, avocado, cranberries, chickpeas, and sweet potato. Sprinkle the top of the

salad with toasted sunflower seeds and the hemp hearts. Then drizzle with the tahini dressing and enjoy!

Vitality Quinoa Salad

This salad is packed full of nutrients that support heart health which makes it truly a meal of vitality. Cranberries and pecans are wonderful for cardiovascular health but they both also support digestion and are high in fiber. Arugula is high in calcium and potassium, also essential for heart and nerve health, and is also high in vitamin C. This salad is bursting with flavor along with vitality, and as it only takes twenty minutes to make and provides for four servings, you can't beat it for a healthy lunch idea.

INGREDIENTS:

- Red onion (quarter one medium)
- Balsamic vinegar (two tablespoons)
- Olive oil (quarter cup)
- Avocado (one medium)
- Pecans (half cup)
- Dried Cranberries (half cup)
- Maple syrup (one teaspoon)
- Quinoa (three-quarters cup)
- Garlic (one clove)
- Baby arugula (four cups)
- Salt and pepper (to taste)

INSTRUCTIONS:

1. Rinse the quinoa in water, then add to a saucepan over medium-high heat with one and a half cups of water. Once it boils, simmer on low heat with the lid on until all the water is gone, and it begins to look fluffy.
2. Remove from the heat and mix it up with a fork and set aside to cool.
3. In a jar, add the oil, balsamic vinegar, finely diced garlic, and maple syrup. Shake well and set aside.
4. Once the quinoa is cooled, divide it into four portions and toss with equal portions of the arugula. Top with sprinklings of pecans, cranberries, diced red onion, and diced avocado. Drizzle generously with the dressing, add salt and pepper to taste and enjoy!

Zesty Beet and Watercress Salad

This salad is packed with nutritious beets and anti-inflammatory ingredients. It can be enjoyed warm or cold and is delicious both ways. It is beautiful to look at and tastes like a sunny fall day. It takes an hour and fifteen minutes to make and provides for two people!

INGREDIENTS:

- Watercress (two cups packed)
- Golden beets (two medium)

- Red beets (three medium)
- Baby spinach (two cups)
- Orange (one medium)
- Pomegranate seeds (three-quarter cup)
- Walnuts (half cup)
- Cilantro (half cup)
- Salt and pepper (to taste)
- Lemon juice (one medium lemon)
- Lemon zest (one medium lemon)
- Olive oil (two tablespoons)
- Maple syrup (one tablespoon)
- Coconut milk (two tablespoons)
- Dijon mustard (one and a half tablespoons)

INSTRUCTIONS:

1. Wash and peel the beets and cut off the tops and bottoms before cutting them into bite-sized chunks. Toss them with one tablespoon oil and a generous sprinkle of salt and pepper. Put on a baking tray and bake at 400F for forty minutes.

2. In a jar, put Dijon, coconut milk, maple syrup, and lemon zest and shake. Add a drizzle of olive oil and a squeeze of lemon juice and shake again. Do this twice more until the juice of the full lemon and one tablespoon of olive oil has been added.

3. Peel the orange and divide into segments then set aside. Wash and toss together the watercress and spinach and layout on two plates to create beds of green.
4. When the beets are done, spoon them over the greens and place orange segments amongst them. Sprinkle the salads with the pomegranate seeds and walnuts, then drizzle generously with the dressing and top with chopped cilantro. Enjoy!

WRAPS – So easy to eat on the go and packed with flavor and health. Wraps are the best for getting the most amounts of ingredients into a hand-held meal.

Heavenly Hummus Wrap

Whether you make your hummus from scratch or buy from the deli, it will ensure this wrap is packed with protein and fiber for a sustained energy release that will keep you alert through your afternoon! Only five minutes to prepare and it provides for one wrap.

INGREDIENTS:
- Tortilla (one large)
- Basil (one stem fresh leaves)
- Alfalfa sprouts (quarter cup)
- Avocado (quarter one medium)
- Cherry tomatoes (six tomatoes)
- Baby spinach (half cup packed)

- Cucumber (five slices)
- Red bell pepper (two tablespoons diced)
- Red onion (one tablespoon diced)
- Hummus (third cup any flavor)

INSTRUCTIONS:

1. Lay out the wrap and spread the hummus thickly on one half making sure to take to the edges.
2. First, lay out the baby spinach and basil, then top with cherry tomatoes (don't cut if it's going to be a long time before you get to eat the wrap to keep it from going soggy), diced onion and bell peppers, sliced cucumbers, alfalfa sprouts, and avocado.
3. Wrap tightly and enjoy!

Cauliflower Spice Wrap with Garlic Aioli

For those that want a substantial wrap they can sink their teeth into and aren't afraid of a little spice, this is the wrap for you. It's smoky and sultry, tender and drool-worthy. It takes thirty minutes to prepare and provides enough for six servings!

INGREDIENTS:

- Tortilla (six large wraps)
- Silken tofu (one package)
- Lemon juice (one lemon)

- Garlic (one clove)
- Avocado oil (four tablespoons)
- Salt and pepper (to taste)
- Avocado (two medium)
- Turmeric (one teaspoon)
- Garlic powder (quarter teaspoon)
- Cumin (one teaspoon)
- Paprika (half teaspoon)
- Arugula (two cups)
- Cilantro (one cup)
- Sweet banana peppers (half cup)
- Sweet potatoes (two medium)
- Cauliflower (one head)

INSTRUCTIONS:

1. Chop cauliflower into bite-sized florets. Peel and dice sweet potatoes into bite-sized cubes. Toss both in avocado oil and turmeric, garlic powder, cumin, and paprika. Place on a baking sheet and bake for twenty-five minutes at 325F. They are done when the sweet potato can be easily forked.
2. In a blender, add silken tofu, garlic, and lemon juice. Blend together until smooth.
3. Lay out wraps and first top with arugula. Add the cauliflower and sweet potatoes, then banana peppers,

sliced avocado, cilantro and finally, generously drizzle with the garlic aioli.

4. Wrap tightly and enjoy!

Taco Lettuce Wrap

Packed with protein and Mexican flavors, this wrap leaves behind the tortilla and embraces the lettuce, making this incredibly healthy and light enough to over-indulge without guilt! They take thirty minutes to prepare and provide for six delicious servings.

INGREDIENTS:

- Romaine lettuce (one full head)
- Cilantro (half cup)
- Avocado (one medium)
- Lime juice (one medium lime)
- Taco seasoning (two tablespoons)
- Bell peppers (one cup)
- Sweet corn (one cup)
- Black beans (one can)
- Red onion (half one medium)
- Garlic (three cloves)
- Salt and pepper (to taste)
- Jalapeno (one medium)
- Avocado oil (two tablespoons)
- Quinoa (one-third cup)

INSTRUCTIONS:

1. Rinse quinoa then put in a saucepan with two-thirds cup water. Bring to a boil, then cover and let simmer until all liquid is gone. Stir it up with a fork then set aside.

2. Heat a frypan over medium and add avocado oil, diced onions, salt, and pepper. Cook until onions are tender. Add finely diced garlic and the cooked quinoa and stir to combine. Drain and rinse the black beans and add those along with the corn and diced peppers.

3. When warmed through, sprinkle over taco seasoning and lime juice and take off the heat.

4. Wash each romaine leaf and layout then spoon the quinoa mix down the center of each leaf. Top with diced avocado, cilantro, and jalapeno.

5. Fold over the end of the romaine leaf and enjoy immediately. If you want to take this as a packed lunch, put the quinoa mix in a container and top it with the avocado, cilantro, and jalapeno, and pack the romaine separately then assemble as you eat.

SANDWICHES – You can't beat a sandwich, it's one of the most popular meals out there. These recipes will show you the variety that eating vegan can bring you.

Portobello French Dip

Mushroom jus, sautéed portobellos, horseradish mayo, caramelized onions – it just does not get any better than this. Forty-five minutes prep time delivers two amazing servings.

INGREDIENTS:

- French baguette (one medium)
- Vegetable broth (one cup)
- Garlic (two cloves)
- Onion (one medium)
- Olive oil (two tablespoons)
- Brown sugar (one teaspoon)
- Yellow mustard (quarter teaspoon)
- Onion powder (pinch)
- Garlic powder (pinch)
- Horseradish (two teaspoons)
- Silken tofu (one package)
- Lemon juice (one medium lemon)
- Ground ginger (pinch)
- Soy sauce (one tablespoon)
- Portobello mushrooms (three medium)
- Dried thyme (half teaspoon)
- Black pepper (quarter teaspoon)

INSTRUCTIONS:

1. Heat a frypan with oil on medium-low and add sliced onion, leaving to caramelize, stirring until browned. Add diced garlic and toss through to cook a little then set aside.
2. Add more oil to frypan and add sliced mushrooms, cooking on medium heat until they shrink and darken, flipping until both sides are done.
3. In a bowl, whisk together vegetable broth, thyme, black pepper, soy sauce, ginger, garlic and onion powders, and brown sugar.
4. Put the onions back in the frying pan and pour the above mixture over everything. Let it simmer until the broth has reduced by half.
5. Cut open the baguette then slice into two six-inch portions.
6. Blend horseradish, tofu, lemon juice, and mustard together and coat the insides of the baguettes.
7. Scoop out the mushrooms and onions and let the broth drain off into the pan. Fill each baguette with equal amounts of onions and mushroom.
8. Pour the remaining liquid into two small bowls and place on plates with the sandwiches. Dip and enjoy!

Chickpea Salad Sandwich

Think you'll miss the classic chicken salad sandwich? Think again with this phenomenal substitute. This plant-based power sandwich will slay your cravings and kill your hunger in one fell swoop. It packs a punch with flavor, texture and nutritional content. Taking only fifteen minutes to make and providing joy for four people, you really can't do better than this gem of a sandwich.

INGREDIENTS:
- Thick cut multigrain bread (eight slices)
- Iceberg lettuce (eight leaves)
- Red onion (eight ring slices)
- Tomato (one large)
- Fresh basil (twelve leaves)
- Roasted sunflower seeds (three tablespoons)
- Salt and pepper (to taste)
- Dried dill (quarter teaspoon)
- Yellow mustard (one teaspoon)
- Dijon mustard (one teaspoon)
- Vegan mayo (store-bought)
- Dill pickle (quarter cup)
- Red bell pepper (quarter cup)
- Carrots (quarter cup grated)
- Celery (two stalks)
- Green onions (three stalks)
- Chickpeas (one can)

INSTRUCTIONS:

1. Drain and rinse chickpeas then mash and smash away all whole beans.

2. Finely slice green onion, bell pepper, pickles, and celery and add with grated carrot to the chickpeas.

3. Stir in vegan mayo, both mustards, and dill. Roll and finely slice basil leaves and add along with salt and pepper and sunflower seeds.

4. Lay out four slices of bread and lightly spread more vegan mayo on each piece. Fold up four lettuce leaves and put on top of mayo. Spoon the chickpea mixture generously on top of the lettuce and press down evenly. Add two red onion rings per sandwich and one large tomato slice. Fold one more lettuce leaf on top and finish with another piece of bread with mayo. Cut in half and enjoy!

The Rainbow Stack Sandwich

Bursting with flavor, antioxidants, raw goodness and fiber, this sandwich is one to enjoy with pure joy. It's easy to assemble and tastes amazing. Most of the prep time is lost in grating your veg, but if you do this ahead of time, you can throw this together in minutes. Total prep time is around twenty-five minutes, and it provides for four sandwiches.

INGREDIENTS:

- Unsliced whole wheat loaf (mostly the whole thing)
- Beet (one medium)
- Carrot (three medium)
- Red onion (half one medium)
- Tomato (two medium)
- Alfalfa sprouts (one cup)
- Chipotle peppers (one small can)
- Silken tofu (one standard package)
- Lemon juice (one medium lemon)
- Avocado (two medium)
- Baby spinach (two cups)
- Sweet banana peppers (quarter cup)
- Salt and pepper (to taste)

INSTRUCTIONS:

1. Slice the bread into extra thick one-inch slices.
2. Peel and grate the beets into one bowl.
3. Peel and grate the carrots into another bowl.
4. Slice the tomato and red onion into rings and set aside.
5. Slice the avocado and season with salt and pepper.
6. Blend the tofu with the lemon juice and add four chipotle peppers. Taste before deciding if you want it spicier and add more peppers if you do.
7. Lay out four pieces of bread and generously smear with chipotle mayo.

8. Layer the ingredients by color, starting with the spinach, then avocado, carrots, banana peppers, beets, and red onions.

9. Spread more chipotle mayo on the other slices of bread and top. Press down firmly to set all the layers in place, then cut in half and enjoy.

Chapter 9: Dinner Recipes

BAKES – The ultimate in goodness and comfort. Bakes are delicious, filling, easy and universally welcomed by all. You will find simple one-dish bakes and one that's for the more adventurous.

Baked Root Veg with Chili

Baked stuffed potatoes are taken to the next level with this amazing dish rich in complex carbohydrates, protein, digestive spices, and flavor. The potatoes are joined by sweet potato and yams and the traditional accompaniments are upgraded to something far more satisfying. This meal takes one hour to make and serves six people.

INGREDIENTS:

- Potatoes (three medium)

- Sweet potato (three medium)
- Yam (three small)
- Vegetable broth (two cups)
- Red kidney beans (one can)
- White kidney beans (one can)
- Diced tomatoes (two cans)
- Black beans (one can)
- Dried oregano (one teaspoon)
- Paprika (one and a half teaspoons)
- Cumin (two teaspoons)
- Chili powder (two tablespoons)
- Celery (two stalks)
- Carrots (two medium)
- Bell pepper (one large red)
- Red onion (two medium)
- Olive oil (two tablespoons)
- Cilantro (one bunch)
- Avocado (two medium)
- Bay leaf (one leaf)
- Sweet corn (one can)
- Tomato (two medium)
- Lime juice (two medium)
- Romaine (one head)

INSTRUCTIONS:

1. Scrub and fork the potatoes and yams. Drizzle them with oil and quickly run over with clean hands. Sprinkle with salt and put on a baking tray for forty-five minutes or until you can pierce easily with a knife.

2. Heat the oil in a frying pan on medium and add the diced onion with the chopped bell pepper, diced carrots, and celery along with a quarter teaspoon of salt. Cook until the carrot is tender then add the paprika, oregano, cumin, and chili powder, along with the finely diced garlic.

3. Put in the full contents of the tomato cans, the bay leaf, and the vegetable broth.

4. Rinse all the cans of beans and drain well before adding to the pot. Stir the pot well and leave to simmer for a further thirty minutes. After this time has passed, get a potato masher and mash the chili to squish some of the beans and thicken the mixture.

5. At this point, you can add the juice of one lime, and salt and pepper to taste.

6. In separate bowls, prepare the fresh ingredients: finely dice the avocado and lightly mash with salt, pepper and the juice of another lime. Drain and rinse the corn and toss with half of the cilantro, finely chopped. Shred the romaine lettuce and dice the tomatoes.

7. Check that the root vegetables are done, remove from oven and slice open to cool slightly. Place in a nice dish

and put on the table with a bowl of chili and all the sides for people to build their own masterpiece. You may also want to get vegan sour cream for this meal from the store. Enjoy!

Autumn Stuffed Enchiladas

Beautiful, creamy butternut squash fills these baked enchiladas with flavor, warmth, and whimsy. This dish is easy to make, so long as you're happy with taking the time to roast some root vegetables first. Prep time is one hour and fifteen minutes, and it provides for three or four people, depending on how hungry you are.

INGREDIENTS:
- Salt and pepper (to taste)
- Lemon juice (one medium lemon)
- Cashews (one cup raw)
- Cilantro (one bunch)
- Roasted pumpkin seeds (quarter cup)
- Corn tortillas (twelve pack)
- Butternut squash (two cups)
- Salsa (one and a half cups homemade or store-bought)
- Black beans (one can)
- Olive oil (two tablespoons)
- Cayenne pepper (quarter teaspoon)
- Chili flakes (one teaspoon)

- Cumin (one teaspoon)
- Garlic (three cloves)
- Jalapeno (one medium)
- Red onion (one small)
- Brussel sprouts (one cup)

INSTRUCTIONS:

1. Soak the cashews in boiled water to cover and set aside.
2. Cut the squash in half and after scooping out the seeds, lightly rub olive oil with clean hands over the exposed flesh. Sprinkle with a little salt and pepper before putting on a baking sheet face down. Cook for about forty-five minutes at 400F until it is cooked through.
3. Heat one tablespoon of olive oil in a frypan on medium heat and put chopped onion in, stirring until soft. Finely dice the jalapeno and garlic and finely slice the Brussel sprouts. Add these three things to the frypan and cook until the Brussels begin to wilt through.
4. Strain and rinse the black beans then add those to the frypan and mix well.
5. When the squash is cooked through and cool enough to handle, scrape out the soft insides away from the skin and put in a big bowl along with the Brussels mixture. Mix well again with the addition of generous pinches of salt and pepper to taste)

6. Put the tortillas in the oven to soften up (don't let them get crispy) while you get a baking dish out and very lightly oil the base and sides before spooning some salsa into it and doing the same. Spoon the squash mixture into the middle of the soft tortillas. Carefully roll them up to make little open-ended wraps, then put in the baking dish with the open ends down to stop them from unrolling.

7. Do this for all twelve tortillas then pour the rest of the salsa on top and spread to evenly coat. Change the temperature of the oven to 350F and bake for thirty minutes.

8. While these cooks put the drained, soaked cashews into a blender with one and a half cups cold water, lemon juice, and a quarter teaspoon salt. Blend until smooth, adding tiny drizzles of water if it becomes too thick. This is your sour cream.

9. When enchiladas are done, leave to cool while you chop cilantro. Then drizzle the sour cream generously over the dish and top with cilantro and pumpkin seeds. Enjoy!

Creamy Vegetable Casserole

This casserole takes you to a new level of pleasure with every bite. So much so that you'll forget that it is packed with whole vegetables. This meal is rich in vitamins, minerals, fiber, and goodness. It takes only one hour to prepare and provides for eight people.

INGREDIENTS:

- Fresh rosemary (two tablespoons)
- Dried basil (one teaspoon)
- Dried oregano (one teaspoon)
- Garlic (three cloves)
- Nutritional yeast (half cup)
- Salt and pepper (to taste)
- Olive oil (two tablespoons)
- Apple cider vinegar (two tablespoons)
- Raw cashews (one cup)
- Zucchini (two large)
- Broccoli (one medium head)
- Cauliflower (one and a half medium head)
- Russet potatoes (ten medium)

INSTRUCTIONS:

1. Pour boiled water over the cashews and leave to soak.
2. Cut up the cauliflower into small florets and boil until soft.
3. The potatoes in this dish will be similar to scalloped potatoes so they need to be sliced thinly. Cut carefully,

but don't be too precise, just so long as they are as thin as you can get them (think really fat potato chips).

4. When the cauliflower is done, drain it and put it in a blender along with the drained cashews and one and a half cups of cold water. Add a good half teaspoon of salt along with the apple cider vinegar and nutritional yeast. Blend until creamy.

5. Wash and grate the zucchini, set aside. Cut the broccoli into small bite-sized pieces and set aside.

6. In a large baking dish, spread the sides and bottom with generous amounts of olive oil. Then put two layers of potatoes down so that there are no gaps to the bottom.

7. Pour half of the cauliflower sauce to cover and spread evenly. Add the grated zucchini and spread out to cover the sauce. Sprinkle the oregano and basil over the zucchini, then push the pieces of broccoli into the zucchini to keep the surface as even as possible.

8. Drizzle a little more cauliflower sauce around the broccoli pieces to fill in the gaps. Do another layer to use up the rest of the potatoes, then pour the rest of the sauce over top of that. Spread it out as evenly as possible, right to the edges to fill in all the gaps around the sides.

9. Sprinkle the top with a half teaspoon of black pepper and a generous pinch or two of salt. Finely chop the fresh rosemary and sprinkle that on top also. Put in the

oven on 400F for forty-five minutes. It will be done when a knife pierces the potatoes without pulling them up and the top should be beautifully browned. Let it cool before serving and enjoy!

Pasta – Italian, cheesy, decadent, lasagnas; all the words that mean love and care and satisfaction. These recipes will help you share the love with your guests and remind you what true self-love is when you make them for yourself. Indulgence doesn't have to be unhealthy.

Vegan Mac and Cheese

Cheesy and tasty with a healthy kick, you will be making this dish over and over again. With only forty minutes prep time, it provides for two hungry people.

INGREDIENTS:

- Cashews (two-thirds cup raw)
- Chili flakes (quarter teaspoon)
- Nutritional yeast (quarter cup)
- Salt and pepper (to taste)
- Dry mustard powder (half teaspoon)
- Onion powder (half teaspoon)
- Garlic powder (half teaspoon)
- Garlic (three cloves)
- Russet potato (one small)
- White onion (one small)
- Avocado oil (one and a half tablespoons)
- Broccoli (one head)
- Apple cider vinegar (two teaspoons)
- Macaroni (two cups)

INSTRUCTIONS:

1. Peel and grate potato and grate. Finely dice the garlic.
2. Heat a large saucepan and oil over medium heat. Put onion and a little salt in the pot and cook until soft.
3. Put the potato, chili flakes and garlic along with mustard, onion and garlic powders into the pot. Stir well until their flavors release, then add one cup of water and the cashews. Keep stirring at a simmer until the potatoes are soft.
4. Pour entire mixture into a blender along with the apple cider vinegar and nutritional yeast, then salt and

pepper. The consistency should be that of cheese sauce that is thick yet runny. If it is too thick, add more water, if it needs more salt or garlic powder, chili flakes or vinegar, do so now according to your taste.

5. Put the pasta on the stove in a large pot with water to cover and a little salt. In another pot, boil the broccoli in bite-sized florets until tender.

6. When both are ready, transfer everything into one pot and cover with the cheese sauce. Combine well, serve and enjoy!

Butternut Squash Alfredo

This recipe surpasses the original alfredo in flavor and also in nutritional value. Butternut squash is a great natural source of B vitamins and vitamin E. It is also an excellent digestive aid and provides beautiful soluble bulk for a healthy colon. The sage is a wonderful antimicrobial and is rich in vitamin A and K. Together, they make this usually guilty-pleasure a valuable dish for digestive health. It takes one hour to make and provides for four people.

INGREDIENTS:

- Whole grain linguine (three cups)

- Vegetable broth (two cups)
- Butternut Squash (three cups diced)
- Salt (quarter teaspoon)
- Paprika (one teaspoon)
- Black pepper (half teaspoon)
- Garlic (two cloves)
- White onion (one medium)
- Green peas (one cup)
- Zucchini (one large)
- Olive oil (two tablespoons)
- Sage (two tablespoons fresh)

INSTRUCTIONS:

1. Heat the oil in a large frypan with medium heat. While it heats, ensures the sage leaves are clean and dry, then put in the oil to fry, moving around to not burn. Pull them out and put them on a paper towel.
2. Into the frypan, put the peeled and diced squash along with paprika, diced onion, and black pepper. Cook until the onion is soft then add the broth and salt to taste. Bring to a boil before turning down to low heat and leaving the squash to cook through.
3. In another pot, cook the linguine in water with a little salt.
4. When the squash is tender, put it in a blender along with all the liquid and other ingredients. Blend until creamy

and taste to see if more salt, pepper or spice is needed. Put it back in the frypan to keep warm on low heat.

5. Using a grater, grate the zucchini lengthwise to make long noodles. Make as many long ones as you can to blend in with the linguine. Add them to the sauce along with the green peas and cook in the butternut squash for five minutes.

6. When the pasta is done, save one cup of liquid before you drain it. Add the linguine to the pasta and stir well to coat the linguine. If the sauce is too thick, add a little of the reserved pasta water.

7. Serve the pasta topped with the fried sage leaves and a little more black pepper. Enjoy!

Vegan Lasagna

Does it get any better than the smell of lasagna? It means you're home and you're safe. This recipe ticks both of those boxes while also being packed full of rich vegetables, fiber, and nutrients. It takes only 90 minutes to make and provides for eight people.

INGREDIENTS:
- Tapioca starch (four tablespoons)
- Salt (half teaspoon)
- Apple cider vinegar (one tablespoon)
- Lemon juice (four medium lemons)

132

- Raw cashews (one and a half cups)
- Baby spinach (three cups)
- Lasagna noodles (one box)
- Zucchini (two medium)
- Garlic powder (half teaspoon)
- Dried oregano (two teaspoons)
- Dried basil (two teaspoons)
- Salt (one teaspoon)
- Olive oil (two tablespoons)
- Nutritional yeast (half cup)
- Firm tofu (one pack)
- Tomato puree (one mini can)
- Onion powder (one tablespoon)
- Garlic (six bulbs)
- White onion (one medium)
- Salt and pepper (to taste)
- Crushed tomatoes (two cans)
- Dried red lentils (one cup dried)

INSTRUCTIONS:

1. Put three cups of water in a saucepan with the lentils, then bring to a boil before reducing to a simmer for around twenty minutes. Drain the lentils and set aside.
2. In the same saucepan, add oil and the diced onion and let cook down. When the onion is soft, add finely diced

garlic, generous pinches of salt and pepper, one teaspoon each of dried oregano and basil, the two cans of crushed tomato and the one can of tomato puree. Leave to simmer for fifteen minutes, stirring every five minutes. Add the lentils to this then set aside, this is the chunky marinara.

3. Put half a cup of cashews into a bowl with two cups of boiled water and set aside.

4. Wash and slice the zucchini into lengthwise strips that are long and relatively thin then set aside.

5. Put one cup of cashews in a blender and pulse until crumbly. Break up the tofu and add to the blender along with the juice from one lemon, one teaspoon each of basil and oregano, the nutritional yeast, garlic powder, and a little salt. Keep pulsing until it is mostly smooth but still a little textured. Put into a bowl and set aside, this is your ricotta.

6. Drain the soaked cashews and put them into a clean blender with the apple cider vinegar, the juice from one lemon, tapioca starch, and a little salt. Pour in one and a half cups of water and blend until smooth. Pour this into a saucepan on medium heat and stir until it becomes stretchy then set aside. This is the cheese sauce.

7. In a large baking dish, place a few spoonfuls of the marinara sauce and spread it to cover the bottom and

sides of the dish. Begin to layer the lasagna noodles, the ricotta, the zucchini, and the cheese sauce. Follow this with half of the spinach, more marinara, lasagna noodles, ricotta, spinach, and the cheese sauce. Keep repeating until all ingredients have been used except for a small portion of the cheese sauce.

8. Put into a 350F oven for one hour on the highest shelf. Remove after forty minutes and spoon the remainder of the cheese sauce over the top to resemble mozzarella blobs, then return to the oven for twenty more minutes. Let rest then serve and enjoy!

CULTURAL – Authentic cultural foods are more vegan-friendly than any of our most recent food trends. Full flavors, aromatic spices, and mouth-watering dishes await.

Creamy, Dreamy Dahl

This dish is so creamy and bursting with flavor that it tastes like it was slow cooked for hours. It only takes thirty minutes to make and is loaded with protein and fiber to keep you satisfied well into the night. It provides for four meals and tastes even better as leftovers the next day.

INGREDIENTS:
- Fresh cilantro (small bunch)

- Lemon juice (half one medium)
- Red lentils (one cup dried)
- Tomato (one medium)
- Salt (three-quarter teaspoon)
- Paprika (half teaspoon)
- Ground cardamom (half teaspoon)
- Turmeric (half teaspoon)
- Fresh ginger (one tablespoon minced)
- Garlic (four cloves)
- Jalapeno (one medium)
- White onion (two medium)
- Cinnamon (one stick or quarter teaspoon ground)
- Cumin (half teaspoon)
- Coconut oil (two tablespoons)
- Coconut milk (half can)
- Basmati rice (one cup)

INSTRUCTIONS:

1. Rinse the lentils then put in a saucepan with three cups of water and cook for twenty minutes on medium heat.
2. Chop the onion and finely dice the ginger, jalapeno, and garlic. Dice the tomatoes too and set aside.
3. Heat one tablespoon oil in a frypan on medium and put the cumin and cinnamon in the oil to release the aromas

for one minute, then add the onions. Let them sweat a little before adding the garlic, ginger, and jalapeno.

4. In another saucepan, fill with rinsed rice, then top with water to cover. Add one tablespoon of coconut oil and the coconut milk (the liquid should be one inch above rice) and give it a quick stir. Cook on medium-high until it boils, then put the lid on and turn the heat down to medium-low and leave to simmer.

5. After a few minutes, put the salt, paprika, cardamom, and turmeric into the mix along with the diced tomato. If you used a cinnamon stick, pull it out now. Leave this on low to cook through.

6. When the lentils are done, drain them and put them back on the stove top. Scrape the tomato mixture into the lentils, along with the lemon juice and salt if needed. Mix well.

7. Check on the rice, and if the water has been absorbed and the rice can be easily fluffed up with a fork then it should be ready. Chop cilantro and top each serving of rice and dahl. Enjoy!

Easy Thai Coconut Curry

It just doesn't get any tastier or authentic than a true Thai curry. This dish is quick to make and packs a huge punch in the flavor department. You can adjust the vegetables and protein to your preference as everything tastes good in this dish. It takes only thirty minutes to make and serves four.

INGREDIENTS:

- Jasmine rice (one cup)
- Fresh basil leaves (quarter cup)
- Kaffir lime leaves (three leaves)
- Whole peppercorns (two tablespoons)
- Snap peas (one cup)
- Eggplant (one small)
- Fresh ginger (one teaspoon grated)
- Garlic (three cloves)
- Lime juice (one medium lime)
- Coconut oil (four tablespoons)
- Maple syrup (one teaspoon)
- Soy sauce (one tablespoon)
- Firm tofu (one package)
- Thai red curry paste (three tablespoons)
- Coconut milk (one can)

INSTRUCTIONS:

1. In a bowl, mix half the can of coconut milk with the soy sauce, maple syrup and curry paste.
2. Drain the tofu and cut into small cubes. Finely dice two cloves of garlic, grate the ginger and set aside. Cut the

eggplant into small pieces, toss them in generous amounts of salt and set aside in a bowl.

3. In another saucepan, put one tablespoon coconut oil and heat on medium. Dice the last clove of garlic and put into the oil along with the rice. Stir around as the garlic cooks and the oil coats the rice. When some of the rice starts to get a little toasted, pour in water to just cover the rice and add the other half can of coconut milk along with one kefir lime leaf. Wait for it to come to a boil, then put the lid on, change heat to low and let it simmer without touching it.

4. Heat one tablespoon oil in a large frypan on medium and put in the tofu, cooking until all sides have been fried and are browned. Set the tofu aside.

5. Put in two more tablespoons of oil and put in the ginger and garlic and let fry for one minute. Rinse the salt off the eggplant, drain and put the eggplant in with the ginger and garlic.

6. When the eggplant gets a little soft and a little color, then add the snap peas and change heat to high. Put the curry mix into the pan and also the tofu and two of the lime leaves along with the peppercorns.

7. Cook for another two minutes while stirring to get everything coated and combined.

8. Check on the rice, it will be done when there is no liquid left and the rice can be fluffed easily with a fork. Remove the lime leaf and spoon rice onto plates.

9. Slice up the basil and quickly stir through the curry before spooning it over the rice. Finish with a generous squeeze of lime over everything and enjoy!

Sabrosa Spanish Paella

Delicate flavors, hearty rice, excellent sources of protein, B vitamins, selenium, vitamin D and vitamin C. Easy to make, but a little time is required for this dish that takes an hour and a half to make but provides for a party of four!

INGREDIENTS:
- Paprika (one teaspoon)
- Cayenne (half teaspoon)
- Saffron (one pinch)
- Capers (two tablespoons)
- Garlic (two cloves)
- Red bell pepper (three medium)
- Artichoke hearts (two small jars)
- Portobello mushrooms (three cups)
- Lime (one medium)
- White onion (one medium)
- Salt and pepper (to taste)
- Olive oil (three tablespoons)
- Nutritional yeast (two tablespoons)
- Saffron rice (two cups)

- White wine (two cups)
- Vegetable stock (six cups)

INSTRUCTIONS:

1. Heat a large soup pot on medium-high and put in four cups of the vegetable stock and all of the wine. Let it boil before adding all the rice, then put the lid on and allow to simmer for fifteen minutes.
2. Turn on the oven at 375F.
3. Put two red bell peppers on a baking tray and cut them in half then rub with olive oil using clean hands so they are well coated. Put in the oven cut side down and cook for twenty minutes or until they get all wrinkly and start to look a little burnt.
4. Get an oven-safe large frypan (if you don't have one, then use a regular frypan and get an oven dish ready for later) and heat a tablespoon of olive oil on medium before adding diced onions and one thinly sliced bell pepper.
5. After the onions and bell pepper become soft, put in the sliced mushrooms and leave for five more minutes.
6. Put into the frypan the cayenne, paprika, and saffron and stir around. Then put in the finely diced garlic, capers and artichoke hearts (without the liquid).

7. When the bell peppers are ready from the oven, let them cool before pulling off their skins then chop them into small slices and add to the frypan.

8. Drain the rice and then put in the frypan and mix well. Add generous amounts of salt and pepper at this point and taste.

9. If you used an oven-safe frypan, then put it into the oven. If you didn't, then transfer the pan contents into an oven dish and put that in instead.

10. After ten minutes, pull out the dish and add one cup of vegetable broth and mix through really well. Do this again after another ten minutes, then remove ten minutes later. The paella should have been in the oven for a total of thirty minutes.

11. Cut up a lime into wedges and scatter about the dish. Roughly chop fresh parsley and scatter this over top also along with the nutritional yeast. Enjoy!

ROASTS – Going vegan doesn't mean you have to give up the traditional roast, if anything, it means you get to experience unique flavors and textures that you never knew existed!

Vegan Festive Nut Roast

Cranberries, Cashews, and Chestnuts make this roast one to die for. It is moist, merry and goes so well with all your favorite sides and accompaniments. It takes two hours to prepare and provides for a family of six!

INGREDIENTS:

- Paprika (two teaspoons)
- Tomato puree (one teaspoon)
- Miso paste (two teaspoons)
- Dried rosemary (half teaspoon)
- Dried sage (half teaspoon)
- Dried thyme (half teaspoon)
- Tahini (one tablespoon)
- Dried breadcrumbs (one cup)
- Chestnuts (one small can)
- Raw cashews (one cup)
- Carrots (one and a half cups)
- Fresh rosemary (two sprigs)
- Fresh thyme (two sprigs)
- Butternut squash (one and a half cups)
- Olive oil (one tablespoon)
- Garlic (two cloves)
- Onion (one medium)

INSTRUCTIONS:

1. Peel and chop carrots and squash into small pieces then boil until they are very tender.

2. Put cashews and chestnuts into a blender and pulse until they are ground but not too fine.

3. Heat oil in a frypan over medium and put in chopped onion until softens. Finely dice garlic and put that in too.

4. Mash the carrots and squash in a bowl then add the onions and nuts. Mix very well then add every other ingredient. Well-oil a loaf sized dish and pack in firmly.

5. Bake at 350F covered with foil for one hour, then take off the foil and bake for another fifteen minutes.

6. Flip it out onto a plate and top with fresh thyme and rosemary, serve with cranberry sauce and mushroom gravy.

Roasted Vegetable Pie

There's nothing more comforting than the smell of roasted foods and pastry. This mean has it all! This pie will remind you of the holidays and encompasses everything that the season stands for. Pure indulgent comfort food at its finest is what you'll experience with this recipe. It takes only an hour and forty-five minutes to prepare and provides for six hungry people.

INGREDIENTS:

- Vegetable suet or vegetable shortening (one cup)
- White flour (one and two-thirds cup)
- Salt and pepper (to taste)
- Cranberry sauce (one tablespoon)

- English mustard (one teaspoon)
- Fresh thyme (two teaspoons)
- Hazelnuts (one-third cup)
- Chestnuts (one small can)
- Butter beans (one can)
- Dried cranberries (quarter cup)
- Mushrooms (three cups)
- Garlic (two cloves)
- Olive oil (one tablespoon)
- Leeks (one cup)
- Onions (two medium)

INSTRUCTIONS:

1. Heat oil in a frypan and put in the finely sliced leeks and onions. Let cook down for five minutes before adding the finely diced garlic. Put in the cranberries, drained and rinsed beans and chestnuts, chopped hazelnuts, sliced mushrooms, mustard, and thyme. Add generous pinches of salt and pepper then stir for ten minutes.
2. Sift flour and a half teaspoon of salt into a bowl and make a well in the middle.
3. Put two-thirds of a cup of water in a saucepan and bring to the boil then stir in the suet to melt.
4. Pour into the well of flour and gently fold the flour in until combined enough to knead. Do so for five minutes then set aside.

5. Oil a springform cake tin then roll out three-quarters of the pastry to lay into the tin. Spoon the cranberry sauce onto the base to cover then spoon in the vegetables.

6. Roll out the last quarter of the pastry and cover the vegetables. Run a knife around the edge of the lip to take off the extra pastry, then press down around the edges with a fork to pinch closed the top and base.

7. Drizzle and rub a tiny bit of oil over the top of the pie before you put it in the oven for one hour.

8. Let it sit for ten minutes before carefully lifting the sides of the cake tin and sliding the pie off the base onto a plate. Enjoy!

Epic Vegan Holiday Roast

This is the ultimate in roast substitutes. Great for Sunday dinner at home with the family and especially for the holidays. It doesn't take as long to prepare as a turkey but tastes so good your guests will think it did. Total prep time is two hours and twenty minutes, and this serves eight people.

INGREDIENTS:
- Salt and pepper (to taste)
- Ground sage (three teaspoons)
- Onion powder (three-quarter teaspoon)
- Garlic powder (one teaspoon)
- Soy sauce (one teaspoon)

- Maple syrup (one teaspoon)
- Miso paste (one tablespoon)
- Olive oil (three tablespoons)
- Pinto beans (half a can)
- Vegetable broth (four cups)
- Vital wheat gluten (two and quarter cups)
- Sourdough bread (one small uncut round loaf)
- Fresh parsley (half cup)
- Fresh thyme (four sprigs)
- Dried rosemary (one teaspoon)
- Dried thyme (one tablespoon)
- Mushrooms (four cups)
- Garlic (five cloves)
- Celery (one cup)
- White onion (one large)
- Barbeque sauce (two tablespoons)
- Teriyaki sauce (two tablespoons)

INSTRUCTIONS:

1. For the stuffing, dice the sourdough loaf into bite-sized chunks and spread over a baking tray. Bake for fifteen minutes at 350F tossing every five minutes.

2. Heat two tablespoons oil in a large frypan on medium and put diced onion and celery into it. When soft, add four cloves of diced garlic followed by diced mushrooms

and another tablespoon of oil. Put in chopped fresh parsley with the dried rosemary, one tablespoon dried sage and the dried thyme.

3. When the mushrooms have cooked down, put in two cups of vegetable broth and generous sprinkles of salt and pepper. After it has simmered for five minutes, use a slotted spoon to pull out all the vegetables and put into a bowl with the bread chunks. Mix through really well then using a regular spoon, add the remaining liquid to the bread mixture until the bread has absorbed as much as it can without feeling soggy.

4. Oil a large baking dish and spread the contents into it before covering with aluminum wrap. Turn oven up to 375F and bake for thirty minutes covered and another twenty minutes uncovered. Set aside then turn the oven up again to 400F

5. In a blender put one teaspoon of sage with the onion and garlic powders. Put in one tablespoon of olive oil with the maple syrup, miso paste and one clove of whole garlic. Rinse the beans and put in along with one and a half cups of vegetable broth and one teaspoon of salt. Blend well until smooth and put into a big bowl then put in the vital wheat gluten and mix until it becomes dough-like. Use clean hands to work it (think of it like making bread) until it feels stretchy and uniforms then knead for another two minutes.

6. Use a rolling pin to roll it out to the size of your baking dish in a rectangle shape.

7. Spoon the stuffing down the center of the dough lengthwise. It should be stuffed so that when you roll it over, you have just enough dough left to pinch it together around the stuffing center. Do this the whole way down until you have a log. The stuffing should be densely packed inside so pack more in from each end if there's room.

8. Roll in oiled aluminum foil tightly and twist each end like a giant wrapped candy so that the roast is very tight. Put into a baking dish and pour the last half cup of broth around it like a bath and bake for ninety minutes but make sure you turn it every twenty minutes so that all sides get a chance on the bottom.

9. You know it's done when it feels firm to the touch much like a cooked meatloaf. Carefully unwrap the foil and put it back into the baking dish with a little drizzle of oil to stop it sticking.

10. Whisk together the BBQ and teriyaki sauces and pour over the roast making sure it is all coated. Put the fresh thyme sprigs on top and cook for a further ten minutes until the glaze gets sticky and darkens.

11. Let it rest for ten minutes then cut into rings and serve with mushroom gravy and cranberry sauce.

Chapter 10: Quick and Easy Snacks and Sweets

SAVORY SNACKS

Cheesy Popcorn

This popcorn is so easy to make and just as easy to devour. Enjoy any time of day or take to the movies with you for a healthier alternative. The grapeseed oil provides a buttery flavor and texture but is not stable enough to cook with, so two oils are required for this recipe. This takes five minutes to make and serves two people.

INGREDIENTS:

- Popcorn kernels (two tablespoons)
- Grapeseed oil (one tablespoon)
- Coconut oil (one tablespoon)

- Pink or sea salt (to taste)
- Nutritional yeast (one tablespoon)
- Black pepper (to taste)

INSTRUCTIONS:

1. Heat coconut oil in a saucepan over medium heat. Put in the popcorn, apply the lid and shake the pot side to side to coat the kernels in the oil. Leave pot still until you hear the popcorn start to pop. Shake the pot periodically to ensure no popcorn sticks to the bottom and the un-popped kernels find their way to the bottom.
2. When the popping begins to slow, get your bowl ready and tip the popcorn into it when the popping has practically stopped.
3. Drizzle the popcorn with the grapeseed oil and toss through, then generously apply salt to your liking, top with the nutritional yeast. Give it a good shake again so the yeast has a chance to stick to the oil, then sprinkle a little black pepper over top. Enjoy!

Veggie Chips

Potato chips beware! You have been replaced by your much healthier cousins and they're way tastier than you! Sweet potatoes are brimming with vitamin A, fiber, and potassium and they are a much more stable release of sugars than potatoes. Now, these are chips you don't have to feel guilty about. They take thirty minutes to prepare and provide enough for two.

INGREDIENTS:

- Paprika (quarter teaspoon)
- Salt and pepper (to taste)
- Olive oil (two teaspoons)
- Sweet potato (one medium)

INSTRUCTIONS:

1. Cut the sweet potato into thin slices by using a vegetable peeler. This produces even, thin, uniform slices that cook very quickly.

2. Put the slices into a bowl and drizzle a little oil on and toss. Repeat until every slice is coated but it shouldn't be drenched in oil.

3. Lay them out in a single layer with no over-lapping on baking trays with baking paper.

4. Sprinkle with salt, pepper, and paprika to your liking.

5. Bake for twenty minutes at 350F, switching the trays halfway through. Be sure to keep checking them to ensure they don't overcook.

6. They are ready when crispy and smell amazing. Enjoy!

Thai Vegan Rice Rolls

These are so quick to make and taste amazing. No cooking is required, and the ingredients and sauce are totally adjustable.

Anything goes! Prep time is ten minutes, and this provides for as many as you like, but this recipe will make three rolls.

INGREDIENTS:

- Rice paper rounds (three sheets)
- Avocado (half one medium)
- Red onion (one slice)
- Carrots (two tablespoons grated)
- Red bell pepper (quarter one medium)
- Fresh mint leaves (six leaves)
- Fresh basil leaves (six leaves)
- Toasted sesame seeds (one teaspoon)
- Crunchy peanut butter (one tablespoon)
- Peanut oil (two tablespoons)
- Soy sauce (one tablespoon)
- Hot sauce (one teaspoon)
- Maple syrup (one teaspoon)

INSTRUCTIONS:

1. Prepare veggies and leave in individual piles on a plate. Slice avocado, bell pepper, and onion into lengthways slices. Grate the carrot, wash and de-stem the leaves.
2. In a bowl, put maple syrup, hot sauce, soy sauce, oil, and peanut butter and whisk together with a fork.

3. Run the rice paper under cool water until all parts have touched the water. Place on a clean work surface making sure they don't touch each other.

4. Layer the vegetables into the middle of each sheet lengthways, leaving a couple of inches away from each end. It should be a log laying in the middle of the round. Sprinkle the vegetables with the toasted sesame seeds. If the rice paper isn't 100% pliable, wait until it is. It should feel like stretchy fabric.

5. Fold one side over the vegetable log, then fold in both ends before rolling up like a burrito. Do this for all three, then put on a plate. Dip the roll into the peanut sauce and enjoy!

DIPS AND SPREADS

Easy Hummus!

Hummus is a rich source of protein, is a powerful anti-inflammatory food and is high in antioxidants. It is filling and low on the Glycemic index meaning it doesn't spike your blood sugar and provides your body with a slow release of sustained energy. Hummus is a staple of any vegan's fridge, and with so many possible ingredients, it's easy to incorporate into your taste preferences. This recipe takes five minutes to make and provides two cups of hummus.

INGREDIENTS:

- Tahini (quarter cup)
- Extra virgin olive oil (three tablespoons))
- Garlic (one clove)
- Chickpeas (one can)
- Lemon juice (one medium lemon)
- Paprika (quarter teaspoon)
- Cumin (half teaspoon)
- Salt and pepper (to taste)

INSTRUCTIONS:

1. In a food processor put the lemon juice and tahini along with one tablespoon of olive oil and the garlic and blend for one minute.

2. Add another tablespoon of olive oil with the cumin and paprika, then spatula the sides clean of the mixture. Drain and rinse the chickpeas and put them into the mix before blending for another minute.

3. Add salt and pepper, the last tablespoon of oil and one tablespoon of cool water and blend again for another minute. Stop and have a little taste. If it needs more of anything, now is the time to do so.

4. On a low setting, blend the hummus again, but put one more tablespoon of water as it blends to make it as smooth as possible.

5. Scoop into a container and drizzle with more olive oil. Enjoy!

Spicy Cheesy Queso

Does it get any better? Hot, cheesy dip for nachos, corn chips, quesadillas, pizza, veggies, fondue – you name it, this queso works! This dip takes minutes to make and will last for four individual servings.

INGREDIENTS:

- Paprika (quarter teaspoon)
- Canned jalapenos (two tablespoons)
- Garlic powder (quarter teaspoon)
- Onion powder (half teaspoon)
- Salt (halt teaspoon)
- Coconut milk (three-quarter cup)
- Nutritional yeast (three tablespoons)
- Tapioca starch (two tablespoons)
- Salsa (three tablespoons)

INSTRUCTIONS:

1. In a blender put the drained jalapenos, garlic and onion powders, salt, coconut milk, tapioca starch, and nutritional yeast. Pulse until combined, the jalapenos shouldn't be 100% blended.
2. Pour into a saucepan, add the salsa and bring to a boil while stirring. Turn heat down to low and let it simmer

until it starts coming away from the sides and if you pull up the spoon, it pulls like a real cheese sauce.

3. Scrape into a serving bowl and enjoy with corn chips or whatever you'd like!

Holy Guacamole

How can any vegan live without the creamy amazingness of guac? It goes with everything, is amazing in wraps and sandwiches, as a dip, on top of salads and as a side dish to spicy meals. Modify this recipe to your own preference. It takes minutes to make and provides for four servings.

INGREDIENTS:

- Garlic (one clove)
- Ripe avocados (three medium)
- Red onion (half cup)
- Lime juice (one medium lime)
- Salt and pepper (to taste)
- Roma tomatoes (two medium)
- Cilantro (quarter cup)
- Jalapeno (one medium)
- Nutritional yeast (one tablespoon)

INSTRUCTIONS:

1. Scoop out the avocado flesh and dice into cubes. Put this in a bowl and cover with lime juice then mash with the back of a fork until it's a little chunky.
2. Finely dice the garlic, onion, jalapeno, and cilantro, then add to the avocado.
3. Cut the tomatoes in half and scoop out the seeds and pulp. Then dice the tomato and add to the avocado along with the nutritional yeast and salt and pepper to taste.
4. Mix together well but not too much as you don't want the guacamole to become too smooth. Enjoy with corn chips or anything else you like!

NUT BARS AND ENERGY BALLS

Happy Granola Bar

Granola bars are delicious, but the best ones are the ones that have little treats hidden inside. This no-bake recipe is easy to prepare and is filled with a variety of flavors and textures. They take fifteen minutes to make and provide you with ten delicious bars.

INGREDIENTS:
- Chia seeds (one tablespoon)

- Cinnamon (quarter teaspoon)
- Desiccated coconut (quarter cup)
- Almonds (three-quarter cup)
- Oats (two cups)
- Maple syrup (quarter cup)
- Blackstrap molasses (quarter cup)
- Almond butter (two-thirds cup)
- Hazelnuts (quarter cup)
- Cocoa powder (one teaspoon)

INSTRUCTIONS:

1. Heat a saucepan over medium heat and put in the almond butter, maple syrup and molasses. Stir until the almond butter has melted down.
2. Take off the heat and stir in everything except the nuts.
3. Using a large butcher's knife, roughly chop up the almonds and hazelnuts so that they are a variety of sizes and maybe a few are left whole.
4. Fold the nuts through the mix and have a taste to see if it needs anything else. You could add some salt or dried berries at this point if you think it needs it.
5. Line a slice pan with baking paper and press the mixture into it with pressure until it is firmly packed down and relatively even in the pan.
6. Put in the fridge until hardened, then cut into slices and store in a container in the fridge. Enjoy!

Peanut Butter Protein Balls

These are no bake, packed with protein and brain-feeding fats to get you through any afternoon. An excellent snack to keep on hand for when you need an energy boost. They take ten minutes to make and provide twenty delicious snacks!

INGREDIENTS:

- Almond milk (two tablespoons)
- Sesame seeds (one-third cup)
- Roasted sunflower seeds (one-third cup)
- Vanilla extract (one teaspoon)
- Maple syrup (three tablespoons)
- Smooth peanut butter (half cup)
- Cocoa powder (two teaspoons)
- Chia seeds (one tablespoon)
- Cinnamon (half teaspoon)
- Chocolate vegan protein powder (half cup)
- Rolled oats (one and a half cup)

INSTRUCTIONS:

1. Put everything into a large bowl except for the almond milk and mix well.

2. Using clean hands, add the almond milk one tablespoon at a time and knead the mixture together until you get a large sticky mass.

3. Roll into twenty same-sized balls, tossing each one in some cocoa powder to coat. Put into a container and keep in the fridge until ready to eat. Enjoy!

Super Seedy Cookie Bites

They may sound like a cookie, but they are disguising a powerhouse ingredient list that is all whole foods, high protein, high fiber and nutrient dense. They take forty minutes to make and make twenty cookie bites!

INGREDIENTS:

- Shredded coconut (one cup)
- Cacao nibs (two tablespoons)
- Hemp hearts (three tablespoons)
- Dried cranberries (quarter cup)
- Raisins (quarter cup)
- Pumpkin seeds (half cup)
- Flaxseed meal (half cup)
- Walnuts (half cup)
- Medjool dates (eight)
- Banana (one medium)

INSTRUCTIONS:

1. Blend the dates and banana into a paste and put into a large bowl with the rest of the ingredients.
2. Mix together well using a little water if it needs help to combine.
3. Roll into twenty equal balls and lay out on a baking tray lined with baking paper. Squish each ball down slightly with your thumb to make a little cookie bite.
4. Cook for twenty-five minutes at 300F. Let them cool before you put in a container. Enjoy!

SWEET TREATS

Bitty Brownie Fudge Bites

The best fudge brownies ever with mostly whole ingredients, loaded with protein and fiber, and gluten-free. We are calling these Bitty Bites because they are so rich and decadent, smaller portions are better. They take twenty minutes to make and make sixteen brownies!

INGREDIENTS:
- Cacao nibs (two tablespoons)
- Cacao powder (three-quarter cups)
- Salt (half teaspoon)
- Dates (two and a half cups)
- Coconut oil (two tablespoons)

- Icing sugar (quarter cup)
- Almond milk (quarter cup)
- Vegan dark chocolate chips (one cup)
- Raw almonds (one cup)
- Raw walnuts (one and a half cups)

INSTRUCTIONS:

1. In a food processor put one cup walnuts and all the almonds, pulse until a fine consistency. Then add a quarter teaspoon salt and the cacao powder. Pulse again put in a bowl.
2. Next, blend the dates into tiny pieces and put in a separate bowl.
3. Put the walnut mixture back into the processor and blend while adding tiny portions of the dates until it looks like a dough. You should be able to knead the dough and have it stick together. If it doesn't, add more dates.
4. Push the dough into a slice pan lined with baking paper then break up half of the remaining walnuts and sprinkle over the top along with some of the cacao nibs and press down to it's compacted and flat then put in the fridge.
5. Heat a saucepan over medium-low heat and put in the almond milk until it begins to simmer then take off the heat.

6. Add the chocolate chips and allow to melt into the milk then add a quarter teaspoon salt and the coconut oil and whisk.

7. Put this in the fridge for ten minutes to cool, then sift in the icing sugar and whisk it slowly to thicken the mixture, eventually whipping it like cream.

8. Spread the fudge over the brownie base then sprinkle with the remaining walnut pieces and cacao nibs.

9. Put back in the fridge to set before slicing and storing in a container either in the fridge or at room temperature. Enjoy!

Healthy Salted Caramel Bar

Yes, you heard right – it's healthy and a caramel bar with salt. This recipe is raw, whole food and packed with protein and fiber. It takes twenty-five minutes to make, involves no baking and provides twelve bars!

INGREDIENTS:

- Almond milk (two tablespoons)
- Maple syrup (two tablespoons)
- Vanilla extract (one and quarter teaspoons)
- Cocoa powder (third cup)
- Coconut oil (half cup)

- Salt (quarter teaspoon)
- Cashew butter (quarter cup)
- Almond milk (two teaspoons)
- Medjool dates (one and a half cup)
- Shredded coconut (half cup)
- Almond flour (one cup)

INSTRUCTIONS:

1. In a food processor put coconut oil, four dates, shredded coconut, and almond flour and blend. Evenly push it into a baking paper lined slice pan and put it in the freezer.
2. Next, using the processor again, put the rest of the dates along with the salt, one teaspoon vanilla, almond milk, and cashew butter. Blend until smooth and add to the top of the slice pan and put back in the freezer.
3. Heat the coconut oil in a saucepan on low and mix in the cocoa powder, quarter teaspoon vanilla with the maple syrup and stir until a consistent texture.
4. Pour this over the slice pan once it has cooled off, top with a sprinkling of shredded coconut, and put it in the fridge for two hours. Slice and enjoy!

Tropical Lemon Slice

So fresh, tasty and zesty that you'll think you're sitting on the beach in Hawaii. These slices are light, simple and minimal but pack a punch of flavor. This recipe takes ten minutes to make, two hours to set and seconds to eat the twelve delicious slices it provides.

INGREDIENTS:

- Coconut oil (four tablespoons)
- Lemon juice (half one medium lemon)
- Lemon zest (one teaspoon)
- Maple syrup (quarter cup)
- Salt (pinch)
- Vanilla extract (half teaspoon)
- Shredded coconut (two cups)

INSTRUCTIONS:

1. Heat a saucepan on low and put all the above ingredients into it. Stir until everything has melted together then pour into a baking tray that has been lined with baking paper.
2. Pack it down until it's even then put in the fridge for two hours before cutting into slices and serving. Enjoy!

DESSERTS

Chocolate Avocado Pudding

This whole-foods dessert tastes just like chocolate pudding you'd buy from the supermarket, except it's loaded with fiber, healthy fatty acids, and potassium. It takes five minutes to make provides four servings.

INGREDIENTS:

- Maple syrup (quarter cup)
- Salt (pinch)
- Vanilla extract (half teaspoon)
- Almond milk (four tablespoons)
- Cocoa powder (quarter cup)
- Vegan dark chocolate chips (quarter cup)
- Ripe avocados (two medium)

INSTRUCTIONS:

1. Heat a saucepan over medium and bring to a simmer the maple syrup and the almond milk. Take off the heat and stir in the chocolate chips to melt then set aside to cool.
2. Put everything else in a food processor then add in the milk mixture and blend until 100% smooth.
3. Spoon into individual portion containers, cover and put in the fridge until set. Enjoy!

Decadent Chocolate Cake

Going vegan just makes some recipes taste better and this is a perfect example. Dairy can mask the true flavors of whole foods, but as this cake is dairy and egg free, the chocolate tastes chocolatier, the moist factor is next level thanks to applesauce and your guests will be blown away by the amazingness that is this cake. It takes only one hour to make and provides for eight decadent slices.

INGREDIENTS:

- Vanilla extract (two teaspoons)
- Almond butter (two tablespoons)
- Almond milk (two and quarter cups)
- Icing sugar (two and a half cups)
- Cocoa powder (one and quarter cups)
- Dark chocolate vegan chips (quarter cups)
- Apple cider vinegar (two teaspoons)
- Vegan butter (three-quarter cup)
- Applesauce (one cup)
- Coconut oil (half cup)
- Salt (quarter cup)
- Baking powder (half teaspoon)
- Baking soda (three teaspoons)
- Raw cane sugar (one and a half cups)
- Flour (two and a half cups)

INSTRUCTIONS:

1. Get a large bowl and sift into it the flour, baking powder, baking soda, sugar, salt and a three-quarter cup of cocoa and stir through.

2. In a saucepan on low heat melt the coconut oil quickly then take off the heat. Put in the vinegar, one teaspoon vanilla, applesauce and two cups of the milk then mix well.

3. Put everything together and mix with an electric beater until it's really smooth.

4. Pour into two 8-inch cake pans lined with baking paper and bake for forty-five minutes at 350F. Check by inserting a knife to the center at an angle, if the knife is clean when you remove it, then it is cooked through. Leave to cool.

5. In a clean saucepan, melt together the vegan butter and chocolate chips on low heat while stirring.

6. In a bowl, sift in the rest of the cocoa powder with the icing sugar, one teaspoon vanilla, almond butter and the rest of the almond milk. Pour in the chocolate butter and mix with an electric beater until thick and creamy.

7. Slice the very top off of one cake to make it flat and spoon some frosting on top. Spread it around before adding the second cake. Ice the entire double-stacked cake with the rest of the icing, starting with the top and then moving the icing down around the edges.

8. Sprinkle the top with whatever you like! Chocolate shavings or shredded coconut, chopped nuts or berries. Enjoy!

Vegan Cheesecake with Blueberries

This cake has it all; an addictive creaminess, a tangy berry filling, and a buttery, nutty crust. This takes only forty-five minutes to prepare and it provides for ten amazing slices.

INGREDIENTS:
- Chia seeds (one tablespoon)
- Lemon juice (three tablespoons)
- Blueberries (one cup fresh or frozen)
- Freeze-dried blueberries (quarter cup)
- Vanilla extract (one tablespoon)
- Maple syrup (third cup)
- Coconut oil (quarter cup plus two tablespoons)
- Coconut milk (half cup)
- Raw cashews (two cups)
- Salt (quarter teaspoon)
- Cinnamon (one teaspoon)
- Dates (two)
- Almond flour (half cup)
- Raw pecans (half cup)

INSTRUCTIONS:

1. Soak the cashews in boiled water an hour before starting and set aside.

2. In a food processor, put the pecans along with the pitted dates, two tablespoons coconut oil, almond flour, salt, and cinnamon and blend to a slightly choppy, nutty dough.

3. Press into the base of a six-inch cake tin that is either a well-oiled springform tin or a baking paper lined regular cake tin that will enable the cheesecake to be lifted out when done.

4. In the same processor, put the soaked and drained cashews with the coconut milk, maple syrup, remaining coconut oil, two tablespoons of lemon juice and vanilla. Blend until creamy, adding a little more coconut milk if necessary. If the filling needs more of anything, now is the time to add it; either vanilla, lemon, salt or syrup.

5. Pour two thirds over the nut base and drop the pan on the counter a few times to let it settle before placing in the freezer.

6. Put the freeze-dried berries into the rest of the mixture and blend to a beautiful purple filling and pour over the top of the cheesecake, dropping as before to settle.

7. In a blender, put the chia seeds, a tablespoon of lemon and whole blueberries. Blend and pour over the top before putting back into the freezer for three hours.

8. Remove from the cake tin before serving and slice with a warm knife. Enjoy!

Conclusion

Thank you for making it through to the end of *Plant Based Diet*, hope it was informative and able to provide you with all of the tools you need to achieve your goals whatever they may be.

The next step is to get started with your pantry and fridge. Decide what you're ready to replace with vegan options and get writing your lists! Get yourself acquainted with the new aisles at the supermarket you may have avoided up until now and start to build your confidence in trying new foods!

Don't be hard on yourself either, this can be a little daunting, to begin with, but once you begin to find new foods that you love, it just gets easier and easier. As your health improves and your body remembers what real food can do, you won't ever look back. This is a new journey that you are taking for your own wellbeing, so enjoy it!

Made in the USA
Las Vegas, NV
15 March 2021